# WORLD WAR II

WORLD WAR II

Other books in the
Opposing Viewpoints in World History series:

OPPOSING VIEWPOINTS®
IN WORLD HISTORY

WORLD WAR II

Don Nardo, *Book Editor*

Bruce Glassman, *Vice President*
Bonnie Szumski, *Publisher*
Helen Cothran, *Managing Editor*

OPPOSING
VIEWPOINTS®
SERIES

GREENHAVEN PRESS
An imprint of Thomson Gale, a part of The Thomson Corporation

THOMSON
GALE

Detroit • New York • San Francisco • San Diego • New Haven, Conn.
Waterville, Maine • London • Munich

106850

THOMSON

━━━━━✶━━━━━ ™

GALE

940.54
WOR

LIBRARY OF CONGRESS CATALOGING-IN-PUBLICATION DATA

World War II / Don Nardo, book editor
    p. cm. — (Opposing viewpoints in world history series)
Includes bibliographical references and index.
ISBN 0-7377-2587-7 (lib. : alk. paper) — ISBN 0-7377-2588-5 (pbk. : alk. paper)
    1. World War, 1939–1945—United States. 2. World War, 1939–1945—History.
3. World War, 1939–1945—Causes. I. Title: World War Two. II. Title: World War
2. III. Nardo, Don, 1947– . IV. Opposing viewpoints in world history series.
D769.W68 2005
940.54'0973—dc22   2004052277

$23.70

Printed in the United States of America

✳ Contents

Chapter 2: Was the Internment of Japanese Americans Justified?

Chapter 3: Was Dropping the Atomic Bomb Necessary?

overall the country remained united and helped make the world safe for democracy.

✺ Foreword

On December 2, 1859, several hundred soldiers gathered at the outskirts of Charles Town, Virginia, to carry out, and provide security for, the execution of a shabbily dressed old man with a beard that hung to his chest. The execution of John Brown quickly became and has remained one of those pivotal historical events that are immersed in controversy. Some of Brown's contemporaries claimed that he was a religious fanatic who deserved to be executed for murder. Others claimed Brown was a heroic and selfless martyr whose execution was a tragedy. Historians have continued to debate which picture of Brown is closest to the truth.

The wildly diverging opinions on Brown arise from fundamental disputes involving slavery and race. In 1859 the United States was becoming increasingly polarized over the issue of slavery. Brown believed in both the necessity of violence to end slavery and in the full political and social equality of the races. This made him part of the radical fringe even in the North. Brown's conviction and execution stemmed from his role in leading twenty-one white and black followers to attack and occupy a federal weapons arsenal in Harpers Ferry, Virginia. Brown had hoped to ignite a large slave uprising. However, the raid begun on October 16, 1859, failed to draw support from local slaves; after less than thirty-six hours, Brown's forces were overrun by federal and local troops. Brown was wounded and captured, and ten of his followers were killed.

Brown's raid—and its intent to arm slaves and foment insurrection—was shocking to the South and much of the North. An editorial in the *Patriot*, an Albany, Georgia, newspaper, stated that Brown was a "notorious old thief and murderer" who deserved to be hanged. Many southerners expressed fears that Brown's actions were part of a broader northern conspiracy against the South—fears that seemed to be confirmed by captured letters documenting Brown's ties with some prominent northern abolitionists, some of whom had provided him with financial support. Such alarms also found confirmation in the pronouncements of some speakers such as writer Henry David Thoreau, who asserted that

Brown had "a perfect right to interfere by force with the slave-holder, in order to rescue the slave." But not all in the North defended Brown's actions. Abraham Lincoln and William Seward, leading politicians of the nascent Republican Party, both denounced Brown's raid. Abolitionists, including William Lloyd Garrison, called Brown's adventure "misguided, wild, and apparently insane." They were afraid Brown had done serious damage to the abolitionist cause.

Today, though all agree that Brown's ideas on racial equality are no longer radical, historical opinion remains divided on just what Brown thought he could accomplish with his raid, or even whether he was fully sane. Historian Russell Banks argues that even today opinions of Brown tend to split along racial lines. African Americans tend to view him as a hero, Banks argues, while whites are more likely to judge him mad. "And it's for the same reason—because he was a white man who was willing to sacrifice his life to liberate Black Americans. The very thing that makes him seem mad to white Americans is what makes him seem heroic to Black Americans."

The controversy over John Brown's life and death remind readers that history is replete with debate and controversy. Not only have major historical developments frequently been marked by fierce debates as they happened, but historians examining the same events in retrospect have often come to opposite conclusions about their causes, effects, and significance. By featuring both contemporaneous and retrospective disputes over historical events in a pro/con format, the Opposing Viewpoints in World History series can help readers gain a deeper understanding of important historical issues, see how historical judgments unfold, and develop critical thinking skills. Each article is preceded by a concise summary of its main ideas and information about the author. An in-depth book introduction and prefaces to each chapter provide background and context. An annotated table of contents and index help readers quickly locate material of interest. Each book also features an extensive bibliography for further research, questions designed to spark discussion and promote close reading and critical thinking, and a chronology of events.

✸ Introduction

The titanic conflict known as World War II began with Nazi
Germany's invasion of Poland in September 1939 and ended
with Japan's surrender to the Allies in September 1945. The Allies
is the name commonly used to describe the partnership of nations
that included Britain, France, the Soviet Union, the United States,
and others who opposed the aggressions of Germany, Japan, and
Italy. The latter three comprised the so-called Axis countries,
whose ultimate aim was global domination.

The importance of this war to humanity and the course of history
was made clear, if for no other reason, by its sheer size and
scope. Nearly every country on the planet was either directly involved
in or profoundly affected by it. Moreover, the death toll
was staggering. The noted British historian Martin Gilbert sums
it up this way:

> The number of those who died . . . will never be known with
> precision. Tens of millions of men, women, and children were
> killed without any record being made of their names, or of
> when or how they died. Millions of soldiers were killed in action
> without anyone recording their names, or marking the
> place where they fell. Many calculations have been made of
> war dead. . . . The Soviet Union suffered ten million deaths in
> action. . . . A further 3,300,000 Soviet soldiers were killed after
> they had become prisoners-of-war. Seven million Soviet
> civilians also died; a death toll in excess of twenty-million Soviet
> citizens. The Germans calculate 3,600,000 civilians dead,
> and 3,250,000 soldiers. The Japanese calculate two million
> civilians and a million military deaths, the largest single toll
> being the 138,890 deaths recorded at Hiroshima as a result of
> the dropping of the first atomic bomb. Six million Polish citizens
> were killed while Poland was under German occupation,
> three million of them Polish Jews. A further three million
> Jews from other parts of Europe were killed, bringing the Jew-

ish death toll to six million. More than a million and a half Yugoslavs were also killed after the German conquest.[1]

It must be noted that Gilbert's summary lists only the groups that suffered a million or more dead, yet it still exceeds 46 million. Some historians suspect that at least 50 million people in all died in what was unquestionably the largest and most destructive conflict in history.

Sharp differences of opinion in political, economic, and social matters caused this enormous and tragic war. And disagreements over how it should be fought divided leaders on both sides. So it is perhaps not surprising that nearly every aspect of the conflict was fraught with controversy and debate of one kind or another. These debates were particularly heated in the United States, which ultimately emerged from the war as the strongest, most influential nation on earth.

Was the House on Fire or Not?

For example, Americans could not even agree on whether to get involved in the war in the first place. After the fighting broke out in Europe in 1939, debates raged in the United States over whether the country should help its allies, especially Britain, in the fight against Nazi dictator Adolf Hitler. Some Americans argued that their nation must take a stand against a despot who, in their view, was clearly bent on global conquest. In contrast, others were confident that Hitler's aims were limited to the European sphere and wanted the country to remain neutral. They thought it prudent to avoid committing precious American troops and resources to what seemed to be someone else's fight.

Whichever side one took on the issue of neutrality, as time went on it became increasingly evident that the United States could not stand idly by and not offer at least some kind of aid to Britain. After France fell to the Nazis in June 1940, the British were the last major bastion of democracy left facing Hitler's rapidly advancing juggernaut. Many Americans felt it was morally wrong to refuse aid to a sister democracy in need. Accordingly, in January 1941 President Franklin D. Roosevelt delivered a pivotal speech to Congress calling on his nation to rise to the role of "the great arsenal of democracy," while maintaining its neutrality. "Every realist knows that the democratic way of life is at this moment being directly assailed in every part of the world," he said.

> During 16 months this assault has blotted out the whole pattern of democratic life in an appalling number of independent nations, great and small. The assailants are still on the march, threatening other nations great and small. . . . As long as the aggressor nations maintain the offensive, they, not we, will choose the time and the place and the method of their attack. . . . The need of the moment is that our actions and our policy should be devoted primarily—almost exclusively—to meeting this foreign peril. . . . By an impressive expression of the public will . . . we are committed to full support of all those resolute peoples . . . who are resisting aggression and are thereby keeping war away from our hemisphere. . . . [I] ask this Congress for authority and for funds sufficient to manufacture additional munitions and war supplies . . . to be turned over to those nations which are now in actual war with aggressor nations.[2]

Enough Americans agreed with this position that aid to Britain and other allies, in the form of the Lend Lease program, soon went into effect. Under this program, America lent arms and other war materials to the Allies, who were not required to repay the loans until after the war. Yet opposition to these efforts remained strong in many quarters. Those who opposed Roosevelt's policy feared that it would prove impossible for the United States to stop at merely material aid; sooner or later, they warned, it would be drawn into the seething conflict and perhaps be consumed by it. Robert M. Hutchins, president of the University of Chicago, declared:

> I believe the American people are about to commit suicide. . . . Deafened by martial music, fine language, and large appropriations, we are drifting into war. . . . We have abandoned all pretense of neutrality. We are to turn our ports into British naval bases. But what if this is not enough? Then we must send the navy, the air force, and . . . the army. . . . [Our] house is not on fire. The house next door is on fire. When the house next door is on fire you do not set fire to your own house.[3]

Neutrality and aid to the allies were not the only issues that divided Americans in the years and months leading up to the entry of the United States into the war. Some Americans claimed that the threat of the Nazis and Japanese was exaggerated; in this view, their regimes posed no serious threat outside of their immediate regions. The opposing view was that these aggressors intended to control the world, so they must be stopped at all costs.

Assault on Hawaii

All of these prewar arguments became moot when the Japanese launched a surprise attack on the American naval base at Pearl Harbor (on the Hawaiian island of Oahu) on December 7, 1941. This event forced the United States to enter the conflict against Japan and its Axis allies. Most Americans, representing virtually all walks of life, closed ranks and supported the war effort. And such solidarity was undeniably a major factor in the ultimate victory of the United States and its allies over the Axis nations.

Yet this concerted effort to defeat the totalitarian enemy did not eliminate disagreements, some of them quite vehement, over various aspects of the war. The Pearl Harbor attack itself was a prominent case in point. Both during and after the war, there was a good deal of fervent debate over whether the disaster had been avoidable or unavoidable. The destruction of most of the American Pacific fleet in only a few hours was a disturbing and embarrassing event that raised numerous questions by American legislators and ordinary citizens alike. Many people wanted to know how such a surprise assault could have occurred and demanded that someone be held accountable. In response to such demands, from November 15, 1945, to May 31, 1946, Congress held hearings on the matter and a select committee issued a detailed report. The overall conclusion of the majority on the committee was that the attack was entirely unprovoked and that the blame lay solely with the Japanese leadership.

Some people disagreed with the report, however. A number of historians and other experts concluded that much of the blame for the success of the Japanese attack lay in faulty American intelligence. Several serious mistakes were made that put the country's security at risk; therefore, the attack was ultimately avoidable.

Those advocating this position point to certain warning signs of the impending assault. For example, in January 1941 Joseph Grew, then U.S. ambassador to Japan, heard a rumor about a possible attack on Hawaii. He passed it along to his superiors in Washington, D.C., but they concluded that the information was not reliable and ignored it. Similarly, in September 1941 the U.S. Navy intercepted a message sent from Tokyo to the Japanese consulate in Honolulu, Hawaii. It ordered the chief Japanese official there to report regularly on the number, kinds, and movements of U.S. ships at Pearl Harbor. The chief of the Far Eastern sector of U.S. Army intelligence received a copy of the message and considered it important. Yet his immediate superiors decided there was nothing to the message and failed to pass it on to military leaders in the Pacific. Beyond the issue of these and other intelligence failures, a small minority of scholars have gone so far as to accuse Roosevelt and his advisers of knowing about the Pearl Harbor attack in advance. In this view, the disaster was allowed to occur to provide a pretext for the United States to enter the war.

Issues Involving Jobs and Women

In addition to questions about Pearl Harbor, many other contentious issues preoccupied the nation during the war years, some of a domestic nature, others concerned with the actual waging of the war. On the domestic front, one controversial topic of debate was the degree of control the government should have over the type of work performed by citizens. President Roosevelt and a number of other leading officials urged Congress to pass the Austin-Wadsworth bill. This legislation would have allowed the government to assign both men and women to whatever jobs it deemed appropriate to further the war effort. The bill was strongly opposed by many prominent individuals and groups, especially those representing organized labor, who insisted that it would create a hardship for many Americans. This opposition was so effective that the bill was killed in Congress.

Several other domestic issues proved controversial, some of them involving American women and their possible roles in wartime. One of the more obvious and far-reaching of these issues was the sudden reordering of traditional social and professional roles caused by a virtual flood of women into the work-place. When millions of American men were shipped overseas to fight, a massive labor shortage was created. And to fill the vacuum, millions of women, most of whom had never before worked full-time outside the home, took over jobs in industry and business. The new working woman was symbolized for many by the image of tough, capable, and proud Rosie the Riveter, a popular character created by the painter Norman Rockwell. At the peak of wartime employment nearly 19 million women of all ages worked at least twenty-five hours a week, and most of them put in well over forty hours a week.

Although a number of men resented women taking men's jobs, the general feeling was that this was a temporary situation and also necessary to win the war. More controversial for many people was the notion of women serving in the military. Some people were opposed because they felt that women could better serve the country in domestic jobs. Others argued that war was the work of killers; in their view, women are not killers by nature. Also, they argued, the thought of women being captured and raped and tortured by the enemy would be too traumatic for most Americans to endure. But many citizens, both male and female, brushed these concerns aside. In all, more than 240,000 women served in the armed forces during the conflict, although they did so in non-combat roles.

Minority Groups During the War

Women were not the only members of American minority groups whose participation in the war effort was controversial. Many American blacks desired to serve their country but faced formidable legal and social obstacles. Responding to pressure from black leaders, who were supported by a few white labor leaders, in 1941 President Roosevelt signed an executive order that banned racial discrimination in defense industries. His administration also ordered various branches of the military to cut back on certain discriminatory policies that had long been in place. (In the navy, for instance, black men had been allowed to serve only as kitchen helpers; and they had been excluded altogether from the air force and marines.)

People celebrate the news of Japan's surrender to the Allies in 1945, which ended the fighting in World War II.

As a result of these bold moves, some blacks were able to serve with distinction in the armed forces. However, their participation remained controversial and divisive, since Roosevelt's policies, though well intentioned, did not erase the deep-seated racial bigotry that was then endemic in American society. Despite the positive efforts of many blacks and some liberal-thinking whites, many black soldiers endured abuse at the hands of their fellow soldiers, and military units remained largely segregated along racial lines.

Even more controversial was the issue of what to do about another American minority group—Americans of Japanese ancestry, or AJAs. After the Japanese attack on Pearl Harbor, unreasonable fears gripped many people living in the western American states (where a Japanese invasion force, if any ever materialized, would come ashore). Among these fears were that the AJAs would become spies or otherwise commit treason against the United States. Exemplifying these feelings were the words of popular newspaper columnist Henry McLemore, who wrote:

> I am for the immediate removal of every Japanese on the West Coast to a point deep in the interior. . . . Herd 'em up, pack 'em off and give them the inside room in the Badlands. Let 'em be pinched, hurt, hungry and dead up against it. . . . Let us have no patience with the enemy or with anyone whose veins carry his blood.[4]

Many Americans agreed with this view. Unable to quiet the hysteria, the federal government ordered that Japanese Americans be forcibly removed from their homes and taken to internment camps in central California, Nevada, and Utah. Soldiers and local police agents confiscated Japanese American property and businesses and cruelly broke up many families. Some people ended up dying in the camps as well. Those against the action called it the most blatant mass violation of civil liberties in American history. They insisted that the internment was really motivated by ignorance and racism. The United States was also at war with Germany and Italy, they pointed out, but no Americans of German or Italian descent had been interned. (In fact, a few hundred Italians and a few thousand Germans *were* rounded up and temporarily imprisoned; but these were all foreign nationals visiting the country, not American citizens in permanent residence.)

Military Concerns

Paralleling the controversies on the homefront were disagreements among the war planners and generals over how the war should be waged. Some felt that the Nazis represented a bigger threat than the Japanese and urged pouring more men, weapons, and other resources into the war's European theater. The counterargument was that Hitler posed no immediate threat to American territory, whereas the Japanese were in a position to strike directly at the U.S. West Coast. (This fear was strongest before 1942 when the Americans delivered the Japanese a crushing defeat at Midway, in the Hawaiian island chain, and put Japan on the defensive.)

Another argument within the military command concerned a proposal to launch a massive Allied invasion force across the English Channel into Nazi-occupied France. General George C. Marshall, commander of the U.S. War Plans Division, advocated that this would be the fastest and most effective way to defeat Germany. President Roosevelt agreed. On more than one occasion he promised Soviet leaders, who urged opening a second front against Hitler, that the Allies would cross the channel in force. In contrast, the British prime minister, Winston Churchill, was at first against such an invasion, saying that Germany was still too strong and might repel it. A number of American military leaders also opposed the cross-channel operation because they thought Germany could be defeated through air power alone. They cited reports similar to the following one issued by the U.S. Strategic Bombing Survey:

> For the first four months of 1944 [Allied warplanes] concentrated their strength on [German] aircraft and ball-bearing targets. During the attacks beginning in February, about 90 percent of German fighter production was attacked and 70 percent destroyed. . . . Freight car loadings fell by approximately 50 percent. . . . All sectors of the German economy were in rapid decline.[5]

Ultimately, the cross-channel invasion did take place on D-day, June 6, 1944. This attack, combined with the continued Allied bombing of Germany, created a one-two punch that eventually brought the Nazi regime to its knees.

The Decision to Drop the Atomic Bomb

Even more controversial were decisions surrounding the most destructive weapon used in the war—the atomic bomb. Fearing that the Germans might be developing their own atomic weapons, the U.S. and British governments set the Manhattan Project, their effort to build the bomb, in motion in 1940. The disagreements over these decisions were not made public until after the war's conclusion. In fact, the Manhattan Project was so secret that the U.S. vice president, Harry S Truman, knew nothing about it until he was sworn in as president in April 1945.

The technical obstacles involved in building the bomb were so formidable that, even with tens of thousands of scientists and workers laboring around the clock, it took years to get workable results. The first atomic bomb was not tested until July 16, 1945, after Germany had already surrendered. The world-altering detonation took place in the desert near Alamogordo, New Mexico, where General Thomas R. Farrell, who had overseen much of the project, was watching. He later called the explosion "magnificent, beautiful, stupendous, and terrifying" and said that the sound of the blast was like an "awesome roar which warned of doomsday."⁶ Three weeks later the Americans delivered a similar weapon to a Japanese target. On August 6, 1945, the bomb reduced to rubble four of the city of Hiroshima's six square miles and instantly killed some seventy thousand people. Two days later the United States dropped a second atomic bomb on Japan, this time destroying the city of Nagasaki. And the Japanese soon surrendered, ending the war.

Almost everyone was relieved that the war was over. But the question on the minds of many people, then and in the years that followed, was whether using such a destructive weapon had been truly necessary. President Truman and his advisers claimed that they had considered a number of factors in making their decision to drop the bomb. A few of these advisers told Truman that using such a frightening and lethal weapon would be morally wrong. They warned that the bomb's blast would be so large that it would be impossible to avoid killing thousands of civilians while destroying a military target. They and others also argued that the atomic bomb was unnecessary. In their view, the ongoing blockade and bombing of Japanese cities had already badly crippled Japan. It was only a matter of time before the Japanese surrendered. One American leader who felt this way was General Dwight D. Eisenhower, commander of the Allied forces in Europe (and a future U.S. president). He said that dropping the bomb was not only unnecessary but also might give the civilized nations of the world a reason to accuse the United States of war crimes.

However, President Truman and his major advisers ultimately set aside these objections. Several American military strategists told Truman that the invasion of Japan would take one year or more and would cost at least half a million American and perhaps more than ten million Japanese lives. Another worry was that the Japanese might fight to the death in the tradition of the famous samurai warriors. It was more expedient and ultimately less brutal, Truman said, to kill a few thousand people with the bomb and end the war quickly than allow millions to die in an invasion. Also, he later remarked, the Americans should not be moved by moral considerations. After all, the Japanese had not been concerned about the morality of their sneak attack on Pearl Harbor and the savage mistreatment of American prisoners throughout the conflict.

Like the Pearl Harbor attack, American neutrality, participation of women and blacks in the war effort, and other war-related issues, the decision to drop the bomb has generated a great deal of argument and debate. Some have viewed these disagreements as divisive. Yet it must be remembered that spirited argument and debate have consistently guided the development of the United States—from disagreements over the wording of the Declaration of Independence to present-day debates about American troops in the Middle East. As the great American historian Henry Steele Commager once remarked, "America was born of revolt, flourished in dissent, [and] became great through experimentation."[7]

Notes

1. Martin Gilbert, *The Second World War: A Complete History*. New York: Henry Holt, 1989, pp. 745–46.

2. Franklin D. Roosevelt, speech to 77th Congress, 1st session, January 6, 1941, *Congressional Record*, pp. 44–46.

3. Robert M. Hutchins, radio address, January 23, 1941.

4. Quoted in Daniel S. Davis, *Behind the Barbed Wire: The Imprisonment of Japanese Americans During World War II*. New York: E.P. Dutton, 1982, p. 30.

5. Quoted in Louis L. Snyder, *The War: A Concise History, 1939–1945*. New York: J. Messner, 1960, pp. 399–400.

6. Quoted in Snyder, *The War*, p. 596.

7. Henry Steele Commager, *Freedom, Loyalty, Dissent*. New York: Oxford University Press, 1992, p. 15.

CHAPTER 1

Who Was to Blame for the Pearl Harbor Attack?

✳ Chapter Preface

On the morning of December 7, 1941, Japanese fighter planes attacked the U.S. naval base at Pearl Harbor. The surprise onslaught killed or wounded about thirty-five hundred military personnel and civilians and destroyed many ships and aircraft. The Japanese people loudly celebrated their victory. One Japanese newspaper asserted that Japan had "reduced the U.S. to a third-class power overnight." If asked, American officials were apt to warn that this judgment was premature to say the least. Within hours of hearing about the attack, Americans of all walks of life expressed outrage and demanded that their country retaliate against the Japanese.

The next set of crucial postattack events took place behind closed doors. President Franklin D. Roosevelt met with his military advisers and members of his cabinet, who swiftly ordered that all American military installations be given heavy guard. They also silenced amateur radio operators and grounded all private planes. Meanwhile, Roosevelt received a phone call from Winston Churchill, prime minister of Great Britain, who informed him that at that very moment the Japanese were assaulting British bases in Southeast Asia.

Clearly, there was no alternative for the United States but to enter World War II, which had begun in Europe in 1939 after Germany's unprovoked attack on Poland. Accordingly, Roosevelt and Churchill agreed to issue simultaneous declarations of war against Japan. At 12:30 P.M. on December 8, Roosevelt delivered his war declaration to a packed session of the U.S. Congress. "Yesterday, December 7, 1941, a date which will live in infamy," he began,

> the United States was suddenly and deliberately attacked by naval and air forces of the Empire of Japan. . . . As Commander in Chief of the Army and Navy, I have directed that all measures be taken for our defense. . . . No matter how long it may take us to overcome this premeditated invasion, the American people in their righteous might will win through to absolute victory.

Following the speech, Congress voted almost unanimously to declare war.

The next steps consisted of the actual preparation for and fighting of what, for all involved, amounted to an ordeal of total war. In a remarkable and historic show of national unity, Americans of all political views closed ranks in an allied effort against Japan and its European allies, Germany and Italy. The United States joined Britain, Canada, Australia, New Zealand, and numerous other nations, all of which collectively called themselves the Allies.

With the war effort driving forward in full gear, the question of why the United States had failed to anticipate and repel the surprise attack on Pearl Harbor had to be largely put aside. Early in the conflict Roosevelt asked a Supreme Court judge to head a commission to look into the matter; and a board of U.S. Army officers also investigated the attack during the war years. However, the findings of these groups did not become part of a public debate until November 1945, when Congress held formal hearings on the causes of the Pearl Harbor disaster.

The final report that emerged from these hearings concluded that Japan was solely responsible for the attack and exonerated most U.S. officials from any wrongdoing. Yet a few scholars and other interested parties continue to doubt this official line. These so-called revisionists charge that the president and others knew of the impending attack, or at least considered it likely, but did nothing to stop it so as to give the country a reason for entering World War II. Though almost six decades have passed since the attack, therefore, it remains one of the most controversial incidents in American history.

Viewpoint 1

"The Chief of Staff of the Army, General George C. Marshall, failed in his relations with the Hawaiian Department."

High-Ranking U.S. Officials Were Unprepared for the Attack

George Grunert, Henry D. Russell, and Walter H. Frank

On June 13, 1944, with World War II still raging, Congress commissioned the U.S. Army to conduct a board of inquiry into the circumstances surrounding the troubling attack on Pearl Harbor in December 1941. The board soon held hearings in which it called 151 witnesses. Following are excerpts from the conclusion reached by the board members, headed by George Grunert, Henry D. Russell, and Walter H. Frank, and submitted to Congress in October 1944. The overall finding placed the most blame on higher officials in the army and War Department, saying that they had failed to thwart the enemy attack because they were unprepared. The board particularly singled out

George Grunert, Henry D. Russell, and Walter H. Frank, report submitted to Congress, October 20, 1944.

Chief of Staff George C. Marshall and the commander of the
Pearl Harbor base, General Walter C. Short.

As prelude to the citation of conclusions the following is per-
tinent:

1. SCOPE: Attention is called to the fact that the record developed by the investigation of this Board contains a great amount
of evidence, both oral and documentary, relating to incidents and
issues about which no conclusions are drawn. Evidence was introduced on these so that anything which might have had a bear-
ing on the Pearl Harbor disaster would be fully explored. The
Board considered that its mission implied the revealing of all per-
tinent facts to the end that charges of concealment would be fully
met. In formulating its conclusions the Board has selected for
treatment only those things which it considers material for a clear
understanding of the events which collectively caused the Pearl
Harbor disaster. The full report of the Board discusses and anal-
yses the testimony in its entirety and must be read for a clear understanding of the history of the Pearl Harbor attack.

2. ESTIMATES UPON WHICH ACTION WAS BASED: The
responsible officers in the War Department and in the Hawaiian
Department, without exception, so far as this Board has been able
to determine, estimated by facts which then seemed to impel the
conclusion that initially the impending war would be confined to
the land and seas lying south of the Japanese homeland, as forces
of the Japanese Army and Navy were concentrating and moving
in that direction. British and Dutch forces were being organized
and made ready to move in opposition. The Philippine Islands
which were in this theater constituted a threat to the flank of the
Japanese force if the United States should enter the war. Supplies
and reinforcements were being rushed to the Philippines. There
was complete ignorance of the existence of the task force which
attacked Pearl Harbor. Intelligence officers in high places made
the estimate and reached the conclusions in the light of these
known facts. They followed a sane line of reasoning. These statements are in explanation, not justification.

The estimate was in error. The procedure in arriving at it was faulty, because it emphasized Japanese probabilities to the exclusion of their capabilities. Nevertheless, the thinking of these officers was colored and dominated by this estimate and their acts were similarly influenced.

3. RELATIONSHIP OF COMMANDERS IN HAWAII: The relations between General Short and Admiral [Husband E.] Kimmel and Admiral [Claude] Bloch, the commanders of the Army and Navy forces in Hawaii, were very cordial. They were making earnest and honest efforts to implement the plans which would result in the two services operating as a unit in an emergency. These highly desirable ends had not been accomplished at the time of the Pearl Harbor attack.

4. INTERCHANGE OF INFORMATION—STATE AND WAR DEPARTMENT: The Board was impressed with the apparent complete interchange of information between the State Department and the War Department. As a result the War Department was kept in close touch with international developments and the State Department knew of the Army's progress and its preparations for war.

Two Causes

a. The attack on the Territory of Hawaii was a surprise to all concerned: the nation, the War Department, and the Hawaiian Department. It was daring, well-conceived and well-executed, and it caught the defending forces practically unprepared to meet it or to minimize its destructiveness.

b. The extent of the Pearl Harbor disaster was due primarily to two causes:

1. The failure of the Commanding General of the Hawaiian Department [General Short] adequately to alert his command for war, and

2. The failure of the War Department, with knowledge of the type of alert taken by the Commanding General, Hawaiian Department, to direct him to take an adequate alert, and the failure to keep him adequately informed as the developments of the United States—Japanese negotiations, which in turn might have caused him to change from the inadequate alert to an adequate one.

The Role of Hull and Marshall

c. We turn now to responsibilities:

1. The Secretary of State—the Honorable Cordell Hull. The action of the Secretary of State in delivering the counter-proposals of November 26, 1941, was used by the Japanese as the signal to begin the war by the attack on Pearl Harbor. To the extent that it hastened such attack it was in conflict with the efforts of the War and Navy Department to gain time for preparations for war. However, war with Japan was inevitable and imminent because of irreconcilable disagreements between the Japanese Empire and the American Government.

2. The Chief of Staff of the Army, General George C. Marshall, failed in his relations with the Hawaiian Department in the following particulars:

(a) To keep the Commanding General of the Hawaiian Department fully advised of the growing tenseness of the Japanese situation which indicated an increasing necessity for better preparation for war, of which information he had an abundance and [General] Short had little.

(b) To send additional instructions to the Commanding General of the Hawaiian Department on November 28, 1941, when evidently he failed to realize the import of General Short's reply of November 27th, which indicated clearly that General Short had misunderstood and misconstrued the ["War Warning"] message of November 27 and had not adequately alerted his command for war.

(c) To get to General Short on the evening of December 6th and the early morning of December 7th, the critical information indicating an almost immediate break with Japan, though there was ample time to have accomplished this.

(d) To investigate and determine the state of readiness of the Hawaiian Command between November 27 and December 7, 1941, despite the impending threat of war.

Gerow and Short

3. Chief of the War Plans Division, War Department General Staff, Major General Leonard T. Gerow, failed in his duties in the following particulars:

On the USS West Virginia *U.S. sailors fight fires caused by Japanese torpedoes and bombs during the attack on Pearl Harbor.*

(a) To keep the Commanding General, Hawaiian Department, adequately informed on the impending war situation by making available to him the substance of the data being delivered to the War Plans Division by the Assistant Chief of Staff, G-2.

(b) To send to the Commanding General of the Hawaiian Department on November 27, 1941, a clear, concise directive; on the contrary he approved the message of November 27, 1941, which contained confusing statements.

(c) To realize that the state of readiness reported in [General] Short's reply to the November 27th message was not a state of readiness for war, and he failed to take corrective action.

(d) To take the required steps to implement the existing joint plans and agreements between the Army and Navy to insure the functioning of the two services in the manner contemplated.

4. Commanding General of the Hawaiian Department, Lieutenant General Walter C. Short, failed in his duties in the following particulars:

(a) To place his command in a state of readiness for war in the face of a war warning by adopting an alert against sabotage only. The information which he had was incomplete and confusing but it was sufficient to warn him of the tense relations between our government and the Japanese Empire and that hostilities might be momentarily expected. This required that he guard against surprise to the extent possible and make ready his command so that it might be employed to the maximum and in time against the worst form of attack that the enemy might launch.

(b) To reach or attempt to reach an agreement with the Admiral commanding the Pacific Fleet [Admiral Kimmel] and the Admiral commanding the 14th Naval District [Admiral Bloch] for implementing the joint Army and Navy plans and agreements then in existence which provided for joint action by the two services. One of the methods by which they might have become operative was through the joint agreement of the responsible commanders.

(c) To inform himself of the effectiveness of the long-distance reconnaissance being conducted by the Navy.

(d) To replace inefficient staff officers.

Recommendations: NONE

George Grunert
Lieut. General, U.S. Army.
President
Henry D. Russell
Major General, U.S. Army.
Member.
Walter H. Frank
Major General, U.S. Army.
Member.

Friday,
20 October 1944.

Viewpoint 2

"The ultimate responsibility for the attack and its results rests upon Japan. . . . [The] actions of the United States provided no justifiable provocation whatever for the attack."

The Japanese Were Solely to Blame for the Attack

U.S. Congress

Almost immediately after the end of World War II, Congress decided the time was right for a full-scale investigation of the Pearl Harbor attack. To that end, from November 15, 1945, to May 31, 1946, the Joint Congressional Committee on the Investigation of the Pearl Harbor Attack did its work and then issued a detailed report. The general conclusion of the majority on the committee, summarized here, was that the attack was entirely unprovoked and that the blame lay solely with the Japanese leadership. Furthermore, said the members of the committee, the U.S. president and his advisers had done everything they could to avoid war. On the other hand, the committee did find that army and navy intelligence had been lax and that the War Department should have kept the Pacific forces on a higher state of alert.

U.S. Congress, *Report of the Joint Committee on the Investigation of the Pearl Harbor Attack*. Washington, DC: U.S. Government Printing Office, 1946.

Conclusions with Respect to Responsibilities

1. The December 7, 1941, attack on Pearl Harbor was an unprovoked act of aggression by the Empire of Japan. The treacherous attack was planned and launched while Japanese ambassadors, instructed with characteristic duplicity, were carrying on the pretense of negotiations with the Government of the United States with a view to an amicable settlement of differences in the Pacific.

2. The ultimate responsibility for the attack and its results rests upon Japan, an attack that was well planned and skillfully executed. Contributing to the effectiveness of the attack was a powerful striking force, much more powerful than it had been thought the Japanese were able to employ in a single tactical venture at such distance and under such circumstances.

3. The diplomatic policies and actions of the United States provided no justifiable provocation whatever for the attack by Japan on this Nation. The Secretary of State fully informed both the War and Navy Departments of diplomatic developments and, in a timely and forceful manner, clearly pointed out to these Departments that relations between the United States and Japan had passed beyond the stage of diplomacy and were in the hands of the military.

4. The committee has found no evidence to support the charges, made before and during the hearings, that the President, the Secretary of State, the Secretary of War, or the Secretary of Navy tricked, provoked, incited, cajoled, or coerced Japan into attacking this Nation in order that a declaration of war might be more easily obtained from the Congress. On the contrary, all evidence conclusively points to the fact that they discharged their responsibilities with distinction, ability, and foresight and in keeping with the highest traditions of our fundamental foreign policy.

5. The President, the Secretary of State, and high Government officials made every possible effort, without sacrificing our national honor and endangering our security, to avert war with Japan.

6. The disaster of Pearl Harbor was the failure, with attendant increase in personnel and material losses, of the Army and the Navy to institute measures designed to detect an approaching hostile force, to effect a state of readiness commensurate with the realization that war was at hand, and to employ every facility at their

command in repelling the Japanese.

7. Virtually everyone was surprised that Japan struck the Fleet at Pearl Harbor at the time that she did. Yet officers, both in Washington and Hawaii, were fully conscious of the danger from air attack; they realized this form of attack on Pearl Harbor by Japan was at least a possibility; and they were adequately informed of the imminence of war.

8. Specifically, the Hawaiian commands failed—

(a) To discharge their responsibilities in the light of the warnings received from Washington, other information possessed by them, and the principle of command by mutual cooperation.

(b) To integrate and coordinate their facilities for defense and to alert properly the Army and Navy establishments in Hawaii, particularly in the light of the warnings and intelligence available to them during the period November 27 to December 7, 1941.

(c) To effect liaison on a basis designed to acquaint each of them with the operations of the other, which was necessary to their joint security, and to exchange fully all significant intelligence.

d) To maintain a more effective reconnaissance within the limits of their equipment.

(e) To effect a state of readiness throughout the Army and Navy establishments designed to meet all possible attacks.

(f) To employ the facilities, matériel, and personnel at their command, which were adequate at least to have greatly minimized the effects of the attack, in repelling the Japanese raiders.

(g) To appreciate the significance of intelligence and other information available to them.

9. The errors made by the Hawaiian commands were errors of judgment and not derelictions of duty.

10. The War Plans Division of the War Department failed to discharge its direct responsibility to advise the commanding general he had not properly alerted the Hawaiian Department when the latter, pursuant to instructions, had reported action taken in a message that was not satisfactorily responsive to the original directive.

11. The Intelligence and War Plans Divisions of the War and Navy Departments failed:

(a) To give careful and thoughtful consideration to the intercepted messages from Tokyo to Honolulu of September 24, November 15, and November 20 (the harbor berthing plan and related dispatches) and to raise a question as to their significance. Since they indicated a particular interest in the Pacific Fleet's base this intelligence should have been appreciated and supplied the Hawaiian commanders for their assistance, along with other information available to them, in making their estimate of the situation.

(b) To be properly on the *qui vive* to receive the "one o'clock" intercept and to recognize in the message the fact that some Japanese military action would very possibly occur somewhere at 1 P.M., December 7. If properly appreciated, this intelligence should have suggested a dispatch to all Pacific outpost commanders supplying this information, as General Marshall attempted to do immediately upon seeing it.

12. Notwithstanding the fact that there were officers on twenty-four hour watch, the Committee believes that under all of the evidence the War and Navy Departments were not sufficiently alerted on December 6 and 7, 1941, in view of the imminence of war.

Recommendations

Based on the evidence in the Committee's record, the following recommendations are respectfully submitted:

That immediate action be taken to insure that unity of command is imposed at all military and naval outposts.

That there be a complete integration of Army and Navy intelligence agencies in order to avoid the pitfalls of divided responsibility which experience has made so abundantly apparent; that upon effecting a unified intelligence, officers be selected for intelligence work who possess the background, penchant, and capacity for such work; and that they be maintained in the work for an extended period of time in order that they may become steeped in the ramifications and refinements of their field and employ this reservoir of knowledge in evaluating material received. The assignment of an officer having an aptitude for such work should not impede his progress nor affect his promotions. Efficient intelligence services are just as essential in time of peace as in war, and this branch of our armed services must always be accorded the important role which it deserves.

That effective steps be taken to insure that statutory or other restrictions do not operate to the benefit of an enemy or other forces inimical to the Nation's security and to the handicap of our own intelligence agencies. With this in mind, the Congress should give serious study to, among other things, the Communications Act of 1934; to suspension in proper instances of the statute of limitations during war (it was impossible during the war to prosecute violations relating to the "Magic" [the Japanese secret diplomatic codes] without giving the secret to the enemy); to legislation designed to prevent unauthorized sketching, photographing, and mapping of military and naval reservations in peacetime; and to legislation fully protecting the security of classified matter.

That the activities of Col. Theodore Wyman, Jr., while district engineer in the Hawaiian Department, as developed by the Army Pearl Harbor Board, be investigated by an appropriate committee of the Senate or the House of Representatives.

That the military and naval branches of our Government give serious consideration to the 25 supervisory, administrative, and organizational principles hereafter set forth.

Viewpoint 3

"In view of all [the] limitations to perception and communication [by U.S. personnel], is the fact of surprise at Pearl Harbor . . . really so surprising?"

The Attack Was an Unpreventable Surprise

Roberta Wohlstetter

Ever since it occurred in December 1941, the Pearl Harbor attack has been a topic of debate among scholars, politicians, and ordinary Americans alike. Some scholars have suggested that U.S. leaders knew of an impending attack and failed to take appropriate action. Others have argued that the events leading up to the attack were complex and American sources of military intelligence were widely scattered and sometimes uncoordinated. Noted historian Roberta Wohlstetter, author of what many have called the definitive analysis of the Pearl Harbor attack (excerpted here), supports the latter view. She claims that many sources seemed to conflict with one another and a number of clues later revealed to be of importance did not appear important at the time. Because the picture American military leaders had of Japanese war plans was not always clear, it is understand-

Roberta Wohlstetter, *Pearl Harbor: Warning and Decision*. Stanford, CA: Stanford University Press, 1962. Copyright © 1962 by the Board of Trustees of the Leland Stanford Junior University. Renewed in 1990 by Roberta Wohlstetter. Reproduced with permission of Stanford University Press, www.sup.org.

able that the United States was surprised and in large degree unprepared for the assault.

If our intelligence system and all our other channels of information failed to produce an accurate image of Japanese intentions and capabilities, it was not for want of the relevant materials. Never before have we had so complete an intelligence picture of the enemy. And perhaps never again will we have such a magnificent collection of sources at our disposal.

Sources of Intelligence

To review these sources briefly, an American cryptanalyst, Col. William F. Friedman, had broken the top-priority Japanese diplomatic code, which enabled us to listen to a large proportion of the privileged communications between Tokyo and the major Japanese embassies throughout the world. Not only did we know in advance how the Japanese ambassadors in Washington were advised, and how much they were instructed to say, but we also were listening to top-secret messages on the Tokyo-Berlin and Tokyo-Rome circuits, which gave us information vital for conduct of the war in the Atlantic and Europe. In the Far East this source provided minute details on movements connected with the Japanese program of expansion into Southeast Asia.

Besides the strictly diplomatic codes, our cryptanalysts also had some success in reading codes used by Japanese agents in major American and foreign ports. . . . [U.S. intelligence agents] determine what installations, what troop and ship movements, and what alert and defense measures were of interest to Tokyo at these points on the globe, as well as approximately how much correct information her agents were sending her.

Our naval leaders also had at their disposal the results of radio traffic analysis. While before the war our naval radio experts could not read the content of any Japanese naval or military coded messages, they were able to deduce from a study of intercepted ship call signs the composition and location of the Japanese Fleet units. After a change in call signs, they might lose sight of some units, and units that went into port in home waters were also lost because the ships in port used frequencies that our radios were unable to intercept. Most of the time, however, our traffic analysts had the various Japanese Fleet units accurately pinpointed on our naval maps.

Extremely competent on-the-spot economic and political analysis was furnished by Ambassador [Joseph] Grew and his staff in Tokyo. Ambassador Grew was himself a most sensitive and accurate observer, as evidenced by his dispatches to the State Department. His observations were supported and supplemented with military detail by frequent reports from American naval attachés and observers in key Far Eastern ports. Navy Intelligence had men with radio equipment located along the coast of China, for example, who reported the convoy movements toward Indochina. There were also naval observers stationed in various high-tension areas in Thailand and Indochina who could fill in the local outlines of Japanese political intrigue and military planning. In Tokyo and other Japanese cities, it is true, Japanese censorship grew more and more rigid during 1941, until Ambassador Grew felt it necessary to disclaim any responsibility for noting or reporting overt military evidence of an imminent outbreak of war. This careful Japanese censorship naturally cut down visual confirmation of the decoded information. . . .

In addition to secret sources, there were some excellent public ones. Foreign correspondents for *The New York Times, The Herald Tribune,* and *The Washington Post* were stationed in Tokyo and Shanghai and in Canberra, Australia. Their reporting as well as their predictions on the Japanese political scene were on a very high level. Frequently their access to news was more rapid and their judgment of its significance as reliable as that of our Intelligence officers. This was certainly the case for 1940 and most of 1941. For the last few weeks before the Pearl Harbor strike, however, the public newspaper accounts were not very useful. It was necessary to have secret information in order to know what was happening. Both Tokyo and Washington exercised very tight control over leaks during this crucial period, and the newsmen accordingly had to limit their accounts to speculation and notices of diplomatic meetings with no exact indication of the content of the diplomatic exchanges.

The Japanese press was another important public source. During 1941 it proclaimed with increasing shrillness the Japanese government's determination to pursue its program of expansion into Southeast Asia and the desire of the military to clear the Far East of British and American colonial exploitation. This particular source was rife with explicit signals of aggressive intent.

Finally, an essential part of the intelligence picture for 1941 was both public and privileged information on American policy and activities in the Far East. During the year the pattern of action and interaction between the Japanese and American governments grew more and more complex. At the last, it became especially important for anyone charged with the responsibility of ordering an alert to know what moves the American government was going to make with respect to Japan, as well as to try to guess what Japan's next move would be, since Japan's next move would respond in part to ours. Unfortunately our military leaders, and especially our Intelligence officers, were sometimes as surprised as the Japanese at the moves of the White House and the State Department. They usually had more orderly anticipations about Japanese policy and conduct than they had about America's. . . .

All of the public and private sources of information mentioned were available to America's political and military leaders in 1941. It is only fair to remark, however, that no single person or agency ever had at any given moment all the signals existing in this vast information network. The signals lay scattered in a number of different agencies; some were decoded, some were not; some traveled through rapid channels of communication, some were blocked by technical or procedural delays; some never reached a center of decision. . . .

An Atmosphere of "Noise"

It is apparent that our decisionmakers had at hand an impressive amount of information on the enemy. They did not have the complete list of targets, since none of the last-minute estimates included Pearl Harbor. They did not know the exact hour and date for opening the attack. They did not have an accurate knowledge of Japanese capabilities or of Japanese ability to accept very high risks. The crucial question then, we repeat, is, If we could enumerate accurately the British and Dutch targets [in Southeast Asia, which Japan was planning to destroy] and give credence to a Japanese attack against them either on November 30 or December 7, why were we not expecting a specific danger to *ourselves?* And by the word "expecting," we mean expecting in the sense of taking specific alert actions to meet the contingencies of attack by land, sea, or air.

There are several answers to this question. . . . First of all, it is much easier *after* the event to sort the relevant from the irrelevant signals. After the event, of course, a signal is always crystal clear; we can now see what disaster it was signaling, since the disaster has occurred. But before the event it is obscure and pregnant with conflicting meanings. It comes to the observer embedded in an atmosphere of "noise," i.e., in the company of all sorts of information that is useless and irrelevant for predicting the particular disaster. For example, in Washington, Pearl Harbor signals were competing with a vast number of signals from the European theater. These European signals announced danger more frequently and more specifically than any coming from the Far East. The Far Eastern signals were also arriving at a center of decision where they had to compete with the prevailing belief that an unprotected offensive force acts as a deterrent rather than a target. In Honolulu they were competing *not* with signals from the European theater, but rather with a large number of signals announcing Japanese intentions and preparations to attack Soviet Russia rather than to move southward; here they were also competing with expectations of local sabotage prepared by previous alert situations.

In short, we failed to anticipate Pearl Harbor not for want of the relevant materials, but because of a plethora of irrelevant ones. Much of the appearance of wanton neglect that emerged in various investigations of the disaster resulted from the unconscious suppression of vast congeries of signs pointing in every direction except Pearl Harbor. It was difficult later to recall these signs since they had led nowhere. Signals that are characterized today as absolutely unequivocal warnings of surprise air attack on Pearl Harbor become, on analysis in the context of December, 1941, not merely ambiguous but occasionally inconsistent with such an attack. To recall one of the most controversial and publicized examples, the winds code, both General [Walter C.] Short [commander of the Pearl Harbor base] and Admiral [Husband E.] Kimmel [commander of the U.S. fleet] testified that if they had had this information, they would have been prepared on the morning of December 7 for an air attack from without. The messages establishing the winds code are often described in the Pearl Harbor literature as Tokyo's declaration of war against America. If they indeed amounted to such a declaration, obviously the failure to inform Honolulu of this vital news would have been criminal negligence. On examination, however, the messages proved to be instructions for code communication after normal commercial channels had been cut. In one message the recipient was instructed on receipt of an execute to destroy all remaining codes in his possession. In another version the recipient was warned that the execute would be sent out "when relations are becoming dangerous" between Japan and three other countries. There was a different code term for each country: England, America, and the Soviet Union. . . .

Barriers to Accurate Perception

Indeed, at the time there was a good deal of evidence available to support all the wrong interpretations of last-minute signals, and the interpretations appeared wrong only *after* the event. There was, for example, a good deal of evidence to support the hypothesis that Japan would attack the Soviet Union from the east while the Russian Army was heavily engaged in the west. Admiral [Richmond K.] Turner, head of Navy War Plans in Washington, was an enthusiastic adherent of this view and argued the high probability of a Japanese attack on Russia up until the last week in November, when he had to concede that most of Japan's men and supplies were moving south. Richard Sorge, the expert Soviet spy who had direct access to the Japanese Cabinet, had correctly predicted the southern move as early as July, 1941, but even he was deeply alarmed during September and early October by the large number of troop movements to the Manchurian border. He feared that his July advice to the Soviet Union had been in error, and his alarm ultimately led to his capture on October 14. For at this time he increased his radio messages to Moscow to the point where it was possible for the Japanese police to pinpoint the source of the broadcasts. . . .

For every signal that came into the information net in 1941 there were usually several plausible alternative explanations, and it is not surprising that our observers and analysts were inclined to select the explanations that fitted the popular hypotheses. They sometimes set down new contradictory evidence side by side with existing hypotheses, and they also sometimes held two contradictory beliefs at the same time. We have seen this happen in G-2 [military intelligence] estimates for the fall of 1941. Apparently human beings have a stubborn attachment to old beliefs and an equally stubborn resistance to new material that will upset them.

Besides the tendency to select whatever was in accord with one's expectations, there were many other blocks to perception that prevented our analysts from making the correct interpretation. We have just mentioned the masses of conflicting evidence that supported alternative and equally reasonable hypotheses. This is the phenomenon of noise in which a signal is embedded. Even at its normal level, noise presents problems in distraction; but in addition to the natural clatter of useless information and competing signals, in 1941 a number of factors combined to raise the usual noise level. First of all, it had been raised, especially in Honolulu, by the background of previous alert situations and false alarms. Earlier alerts, as we have seen, had centered attention on local sabotage and on signals supporting the hypothesis of a probable Japanese attack on Russia. Second, in both Honolulu and Washington, individual reactions to danger had been numbed, or at least dulled, by the continuous international tension.

A third factor that served to increase the natural noise level was the positive effort made by the enemy to keep the relevant signals quiet. The Japanese security system was an important and successful block to perception. It was able to keep the strictest cloak of secrecy around the Pearl Harbor attack and to limit knowledge only to those closely associated with the details of military and naval planning. In the Japanese Cabinet only the Navy Minister and the Army Minister (who was also Prime Minister) knew of the plan before the task force left its final port of departure. In addition to keeping certain signals quiet, the enemy tried to create noise, and sent false signals into our information system by carrying on elaborate "spoofs." False radio traffic made us believe that certain ships were maneuvering near the mainland of Japan. The Japanese also sent to individual commanders false war plans for Chinese targets, which were changed only at the last moment to bring them into line with the Southeastern movement.

A fifth barrier to accurate perception was the fact that the relevant signals were subject to change, often very sudden change. This was true even of the so-called static intelligence, which included data on capabilities and the composition of military forces. In the case of our 1941 estimates of the infeasibility of torpedo attacks in the shallow waters of Pearl Harbor, or the underestimation of the range and performance of the Japanese Zero, the changes happened too quickly to appear in an intelligence estimate.

Sixth, our own security system sometimes prevented the communication of signals. It confronted our officers with the problem of trying to keep information from the enemy without keeping it from each other. . . . Only a very few key individuals saw these secret messages, and they saw them only briefly. They had no opportunity or time to make a critical review of the material, and each one assumed that others who had seen it would arrive at identical interpretations. . . . Admiral Stark, for example, thought Admiral Kimmel was reading all of MAGIC [the name given by American intelligence to Japan's secret codes]. Those who were not on the list of recipients, but who had learned somehow of the existence of the decodes, were sure that they contained military as well as diplomatic information and believed that the contents were much fuller and more precise than they actually were. The effect of carefully limiting the reading and discussion of MAGIC, which was certainly necessary to safeguard the secret of our knowledge of the code, was thus to reduce this group of signals to the point where they were scarcely heard.

To these barriers of noise and security we must add the fact that the necessarily precarious character of intelligence information and predictions was reflected in the wording of instructions to take action. The warning messages were somewhat vague and ambiguous. Enemy moves are often subject to reversal on short notice, and this was true for the Japanese. They had plans for canceling their attacks on American possessions in the Pacific up to 24 hours before the time set for attack. A full alert in the Hawaiian Islands, for example, was one condition that might have caused the Pearl Harbor task force to return to Japan on December 5 or 6. The fact that intelligence predictions must be based on moves that are almost always reversible makes understandable the reluctance of the intelligence analyst to make bold assertions. . . .

Last but not least we must also mention the blocks to perception and communication inherent in any large bureaucratic organization, and those that stemmed from intraservice and interservice rivalries. The most glaring example of rivalry in the Pearl Harbor case was that between Naval War Plans and Naval Intelligence. A general prejudice against intellectuals and specialists, not confined to the military but unfortunately widely held in America, also made it difficult for intelligence experts to be heard. . . .

The Far Eastern code analysts, for example, were believed to be too immersed in the "Oriental point of view" [i.e., concerns about Asia and its problems]. Low budgets for American Intelligence departments reflected the low prestige of this activity, whereas in England, Germany, and Japan, 1941 budgets reached a height that was regarded by the American Congress as quite beyond reason.

No Magic to Provide Certainty

In view of all these limitations to perception and communication, is the fact of surprise at Pearl Harbor, then, really so surprising? . . .

Pearl Harbor is not an isolated catastrophe. It can be matched by many examples of effective surprise attack. The German attack on Russia in the summer of 1941 was preceded by a flood of signals, the massing of troops, and even direct warnings to Russia by the governments of the United States and the United Kingdom, both of whom had been correctly informed about the imminence of the onslaught. Yet it achieved total surprise. Soviet arguments current today that [Soviet leader Joseph] Stalin and Marshal Zhukov, his Chief of the General Staff, knew and failed to act have obvious parallels with the accusations about President [Franklin] Roosevelt's conspiracy of silence. These Soviet reinterpretations of history aim not only to downgrade Stalin, but also to establish that Soviet leaders were not *really* surprised in 1941, and the Soviet Union can therefore count on adequate warning in any future conflict. But the difficulties of discerning a surprise attack on oneself apply equally to totalitarian and democratic states.

The stunning tactical success of the Japanese attack on the British at Singapore [in December 1941] was made possible by the deeply held British faith in the impregnability of that fortress. As Captain [Russell] Grenfell put it, newspapers and statesmen like their fortresses to be impregnable. "Every fortress," he wrote, "that has come into the news in my lifetime—Port Arthur, Tsing Tao, the great French defensive system of the Maginot Line—has been popularly described as impregnable before it has been attacked. . . . One way or another it became a virtually accepted fact in Britain and the Dominions that Singapore was an impregnable bastion of Imperial security." Yet the defenses of Singapore were rendered useless by military surprise in the form of an attack from an unexpected, northerly direction. . . .

In short, the subject of surprise attack continues to be of vital concern. This fact has been suggested by the great debate among the powers on arms control and on the possibilities of using limitation and inspection arrangements to guard against surprise attack. The very little we have said suggests that such arrangements present formidable difficulties. . . .

It is only human to want some unique and univocal signal, to want a guarantee from intelligence, an unambiguous substitute for a formal declaration of war. This is surely the unconscious motivation of all the rewriting of Pearl Harbor history. . . .

But we have seen how drastically such an interpretation oversimplifies the task of the analyst and decisionmaker. If the study of Pearl Harbor has anything to offer for the future, it is this: We have to accept the fact of uncertainty and learn to live with it. No magic, in code or otherwise, will provide certainty. Our plans must work without it.

Viewpoint 4

"[Lt. Gen. Walter C. Short] failed to alert his forces to the probability of a surprise Japanese attack [and] failed to follow Washington's orders to conduct reconnaissance before the attack."

The Disaster Resulted from Preventable Intelligence Failures

Henry C. Clausen and Bruce Lee

In this powerfully stated essay, attorney Henry C. Clausen and military historian Bruce Lee make the case that the Pearl Harbor attack was the net result of a series of unforgivable blunders made by American commanders and intelligence officials in December 1941. Clausen had access to much information that other researchers did not because Secretary of War Henry L. Stimson asked him to look into the Pearl Harbor fiasco and gave him unprecedented access to U.S. military personnel and materials. Clausen and Lee rate the people involved on a ten-point scale, in each case charging that the person in question should have known better and should be held accountable by posterity. Clausen and Lee clearly do not agree with the theory that the disaster was unavoidable, remarking, "There was no valid reason for our forces to have been surprised" by the

Japanese. (Clausen and Lee make several references to "Magic," the name given by U.S. intelligence officials to Japan's secret codes; to "Purple," the *most* secret of those codes; and to the so-called "Fourteen-point Message" document, handed to U.S. diplomats the day before the Pearl Harbor attack, which condemned recent U.S. policy in Southeast Asia.)

The proximate cause or guilt for the disaster at Pearl Harbor was an unworkable system of military intelligence, including the fact that the Navy withheld from the Army vital intelligence information that called for Army action.

In turn, this can be translated into guilt that can be charged against individuals. I shall list these people in terms of their culpability, based on a scale of zero to ten, with ten being the high end of the scale.

10. *Lt. Gen. Walter C. Short:* His was the primary duty and task of defending the fleet and Hawaii from attack. He didn't want the command. He failed to study what the task entailed before he took command. He failed to alert his forces to the probability of a surprise Japanese attack. He failed to follow Washington's orders to conduct reconnaissance before the attack. He failed to communicate with his counterpart, Admiral Kimmel, and determine the Navy's state of readiness before the attack. If Short's fighter planes and antiaircraft guns had fired on the first Japanese plane they saw, or the second one, Short would have been a hero even if a large number of the fleet's ships were sunk. As it was, his planes were on the ground and the ammunition for his antiaircraft guns was locked away. It took nearly four hours for his command to get ready to fight.

10. *Admiral Husband E. Kimmel:* As the Commander in Chief of the U.S. Pacific Fleet, he also would have been a hero if he had gone to sea with his ships and been ready to fight. As it was, he withheld vital intelligence information not only from Short, but from his own command. . . . Kimmel also knew from two dispatches from Washington on December 3 that the Japanese were destroying their codes and code machines. He failed to tell Short.

Nor did he ask Washington for clarification of what Washington really knew or what Washington wanted him to do. So, Kimmel is off in left field, all by himself, saying that the intelligence he received either wasn't important or wasn't given to him.

He was a man who was inflexible in his convictions and expressions. He believed that what he assumed was correct. He would not liaise with the Army about its state of readiness. Take, for example, the [proof] that Kimmel did not play fair and square with Short. It does no good to say, "Oh, Short's subordinate had that information." That is not exchanging information. That is partially exchanging information. Kimmel was required to give Short the identical information that the Office of Naval Intelligence in Washington gave Kimmel. The obligation was for one commander to confer and exchange information with his fellow commander. That was the only way the two commands could survive in an era of mutual dependency. Thus, Short became one of the first victims of the Navy's practice of hoarding secret information. . . .

I believe today, now that the partisan political dust has settled, no jury would declare these men innocent. They were obviously guilty.

As for those individuals who should be charged with *contributory negligence*, I list the following: . . .

9. *Col. Carlisle Clyde Dusenbury*, Assistant in the Far East Section of Army G-2 (Intelligence) in Washington: . . . Dusenbury swore in his affidavit to me that he had all fourteen parts of the fourteen-part Japanese diplomatic message in his possession around midnight of December 6, 1941. (I will speak of this again.) Dusenbury had been ordered to deliver this latest Magic material to General [George C.] Marshall at his quarters when Dusenbury went home for the night. He did not do so.

I believe that had Marshall received that night the fourteen-part message, in which it was made clear that diplomatic relations between Washington and Tokyo were going to be broken off, he would have sent a special alert to Short in time to blunt or repel the Japanese attack. As it stood, Dusenbury lost approximately nine crucial hours of this warning time.

8. *Lt. Col. Kendall J. Fielder*, G-2 (Intelligence) of the Hawaiian Department: Fielder represented all that was wrong with the

Army's intelligence system. . . . He was an infantry officer. Although a graduate of West Point, he had no intelligence training. He was not cleared for Top Secret, Magic-type information. He was chosen for his job because of his social graces—golfing skills, a smiling demeanor and magic shows—not for his military intelligence skills. He required that his subordinates do the major portion of his work. He shunned responsibility; he failed to find out what was really going on in the intelligence world within the Hawaiian Army and Navy commands. His was a sorry list of qualifications. As one result, Short paid the supreme price.

8. *Lt. Col. George W. Bicknell*, Assistant G-2 for the Hawaiian Department: When I first talked to Bicknell, I thought well of him. It wasn't until I carefully studied the record and placed one item of evidence alongside the other that Bicknell's failures became apparent. Trained in intelligence during World War I, Bicknell was recalled to duty as a reserve officer and had been shunted aside when Short appointed Fielder to be Bicknell's boss. Yet, it was Bicknell whom the Navy and FBI trusted with secret information, because he was a true intelligence officer. Working against him, however, was the fact that he dealt with, but was *not* cleared for, Top Secret, Magic-type intelligence. Thus, the system placed Bicknell in an untenable position.

Bicknell could have absolved himself. He could have saved the day at Pearl Harbor.

He had been able to [learn] on December 3 at least one of two all-important warnings from Naval intelligence in Washington advising Kimmel that the Japanese embassies and consulates around the world, including in Washington, were burning their codes and . . . destroying their code machines.

Bicknell had every reason in the world to rush to Short with this priceless, earthshaking dispatch. I can only speculate as to why he didn't. He knew that Rochefort had broken security regulations in showing him this Magic information. He also knew that he could get into serious trouble if he revealed the source of his information, which he had been tapping for some time. Instead, Bicknell chose to wait three days and reveal this information in a watered-down form at the weekly staff conference, where he masked its importance by reducing the source to dull routine. . . .

8. *Capt. Edwin T. Layton*, Fleet Intelligence Officer, Pacific Fleet: It's odd. When you look at the list of Kimmel's staff as drawn up by Congress, Layton's name is missing. His name is also missing from the table of organization for the Fourteenth Naval District in Hawaii. Perhaps it was the Navy's way of saying that the Pacific Fleet did not have an intelligence officer. Yet, Layton was there. He even called his book *And I Was There*. In it, he claimed that internal feuding in the Navy Department in Washington was responsible for Pearl Harbor. As it turned out, this was only partially true. What Layton really did and didn't do illustrates the slippery nature of the intelligence specialist: He suckered the Army.

Layton failed to follow Kimmel's direct order to personally deliver the "war warning" message of November 27 to General Short.

Layton also tried to pull a snow job on me during my investigation.

He claimed that he passed vital intelligence information to Fielder in the best traditions of military cooperation. When I brought Fielder with me to Guam, Layton met him with a big grin, saying, "Wooch! [Fielder's nickname] Glad to see you, Wooch." But in his affidavit to me, Layton had to admit that he never had any professional contact with Fielder.

According to the rules of the Joint Action Agreement and the concept of codependency, Layton was required to keep Fielder abreast of intelligence matters. And if Layton was worried that Fielder did not have the proper security clearance for this information, he should have asked Washington how to handle it. He might have suggested liaison with Bicknell. (That might have made the system more workable.)

Layton should not have pretended that Col. Edward W. Raley, who was in charge of intelligence for the Hawaiian Air Force, was Fielder's surrogate. Nor should he have divulged to Raley intelligence information based on Magic without telling him its proper source.

When the Navy Department warned Kimmel on December 3 that the Japanese were burning their codes and destroying their Purple code machines, Kimmel called Layton to his office to find out what Purple was. Layton didn't know. He had to ask a young officer fresh from Washington to find out that Purple was the supersecret Japanese electronic code machine, the most priceless item of Japanese intelligence in existence.

Layton should have known the implications of the December 3 warnings: War was imminent and unavoidable. Layton failed to communicate this point to Kimmel.

Like Kimmel, Layton would never acknowledge that he had made a mistake. . . .

There is no truth to Layton's claim that he was prohibited from passing intelligence to the Army. As General Marshall and Secretary [of war Henry] Stimson pointed out in their testimony, Kimmel and Short, with reference to their respective commands, were dependent upon each other to share *all* intelligence. It never happened. Layton has hidden behind Kimmel's epaulettes ever since.

8. *Rear Adm. Richmond K. Turner*, head of the Navy's War Plans Division in Washington: To understand the contributory negligence of Kelly Turner, one must comprehend that, in the Navy's table of organization, the War Plans Division was the most senior, or dominant, division. Turner was not a man willing to play second fiddle to anyone, including his boss, the Chief of Naval Operations, Adm. Harold R. Stark, who was nicknamed "Betty."

It was Congress that uncovered the problems within the Navy Department. Turner believed that he should be the one to interpret Naval intelligence, since he was sending out the orders to the Navy commanders overseas. This destroyed the efficiency of Rear Adm. Theodore S. Wilkinson and his Intelligence Division. It also kept Capt. Arthur H. McCollum of the Far Eastern Section of the Intelligence Division uninformed of the instructions sent to the fleet based on intelligence matters.

In brief, if Turner had not tried to seize control of the Navy Department while head of the War Plans Division, there is every chance that the Navy would have been better run. . . .

7. *Capt. L.F. Safford*, head of the Security (Intelligence) Section of the Navy Department's Communications Division: . . . Safford was a strange duck. He was in overall charge of the Navy's hyperactive code-breaking activities in Washington. He testified that he was pretty sure that something was going to pop on the weekend of December 6–7, 1941, but he went home early that Saturday afternoon. He claimed he was totally worn out. He was in his paja-

mas, having breakfast in the early afternoon (Washington time) on Sunday when he heard that the Japanese had attacked Pearl Harbor. His immediate reaction was that someone in a high place had blown the call. He never came to grips with the fact that if he had remained on duty, knowing and suspecting what he did, he could have prevented the call from being blown.

7. *Capt. Irving H. Mayfield*, Intelligence Officer, Fourteenth Naval District, Hawaii: He broke the law to illegally tap the telephones of the Japanese consulate in Hawaii for some twenty-two months. Then, in a fit of pique, he broke off the taps without telling anyone so that surveillance could be continued in the five crucial days before Pearl Harbor. I believe that if the taps had been continued, there might have been yet another opportunity to avoid Pearl Harbor.

7. *Col. Rufus S. Bratton*, Chief of the Far Eastern Section of G-2 (Intelligence) in Washington: Bratton failed to assure that his deputy (Dusenbury) followed his orders to deliver the crucial fourteen-part Japanese decrypt to Marshall on the night of December 6. For his part, Bratton believed the material to be so important that he rushed the first thirteen parts of it to the office of the Secretary of State. But then he went home to bed!

Later, he misled the Army Pearl Harbor Board when he lied about what he had really done that night. His false testimony wounded Marshall a second time, nearly mortally. In so doing, he lost his chance for a general's star. But I discovered, and Bratton candidly confirmed, the truth of what happened, including his perjury. . . .

6. *Comdr. Joseph J. Rochefort*, Chief of the Communications Security (Intelligence) Unit, Fourteenth Naval District, Hawaii: It became known on December 3 that the Japanese Consul in Hawaii had destroyed all but one of Japan's code systems. Rochefort failed to realize the significance of the fact that the Japanese consulate in Hawaii could communicate with Tokyo via only this commercial cable system, which he was capable of cracking. He failed to relay the importance of this development to Layton. He also failed to exert maximum effort to crack this traffic. If he had done so, Rochefort would have discovered, as was found out after the attack, that Pearl Harbor had been classified as a target.

6. *Brig. Gen. Leonard T. Gerow*: As head of the Army's War Plans

Division, Gerow bore the responsibility for allowing Short's ambiguous reply about the improper state of alert for the Hawaiian command to slip through the safety net unchecked.

6. *Lt. Comdr. Alwin D. Kramer* (on loan from the Far Eastern Section, Intelligence Division) of the Translation Section of the Navy's Communications Division in Washington: Kramer worked under Safford's direction. What was more important, however, was that Kramer had the job in the Navy similar to Dusenbury's and Bratton's in the Army. There was only one Kramer, however, which meant that there was a horrific chance that something might go wrong if he was not available to deliver material to Admiral Stark or President Roosevelt. The President of the United States had designated the Navy to bring him the Magic decrypts. The Navy foolishly designated only one man to do the job: Kramer.

I believe you can begin to see the problem that has bothered me for years: What happened when Kramer was home asleep?

On the evening of December 6, 1941, Kramer made his rounds and delivered, he claimed, the first thirteen parts of the fourteen-part diplomatic message to the White House. His wife drove the car for him that evening. He finished his last delivery to top-ranking Naval officers and, he claimed, checked in at his office. There was nothing else in the hopper. He claimed he left orders with the watch officer that he was to be called if any important messages related to the fourteen-part message came in or if a message was intercepted saying when the fourteen-part message was to be delivered. Kramer then went home to bed.

At the first minute past midnight of December 6, or 00:01 hours December 7, the responsibility to handle Magic traffic fell to the Navy. That was how the crazy system worked: the Army was responsible for Magic on the even-numbered days, the Navy on odd-numbered days.

So, here we were: The Navy was responsible for handling the decrypts, and the only man in the Navy responsible for translating them was home in bed! . . .

Congress never investigated this adequately. The Committee never questioned Dusenbury, or Rowlett, or Mary J. Dunning, which means that the affidavit Dusenbury gave me must be accepted as true. The Committee never cross-examined Kramer about the conflict between his testimony and that of Dusenbury. Why? Because when the Committee got to this particular issue, its work became sloppy. Besides, no one wanted to prove that the way the Army and Navy had divvied up the distribution of Magic intelligence was more like a comic opera than good intelligence work.

After the Army refused for reasons of security to send the Japanese decrypts to the White House, Roosevelt specifically designated the Navy to provide him with Magic. The Navy failed to do so at a crucial moment in history. Now, the analogy between the failure of the Navy to deliver an important document to the head of state and the Navy's reluctance to divulge intelligence to the Army may seem tenuous, but it isn't.

That is why I conclude my list of those who bore contributory negligence for Pearl Harbor as follows:

5. *President Franklin D. Roosevelt:* I cannot walk away from my investigation and say that Roosevelt was innocent in the matter of Pearl Harbor.

I didn't find any evidence that would have linked him to a conspiracy to force Japan to attack Pearl Harbor. Nor can I accuse him of having more knowledge of what might happen at Pearl Harbor than other people possessed. After all, there were a number of others who read the first thirteen parts of the fourteen-part diplomatic message around midnight on December 6, 1941. Among them were Secretary of State [Cordell] Hull, Secretary of the Navy [Frank] Knox, Chief of Naval Operations Stark, and the intelligence chiefs of the Navy and the Army. . . . None of them foresaw what Roosevelt did when he read the message and told his assistant, Harry Hopkins, "This means war!"

The question of contributory negligence on the part of the President comes down to what Roosevelt did, or did not do, after making that momentous statement some sixteen hours before the Japanese attacked.

His men were looking for leadership at a crucial moment. He did not provide it. Roosevelt made a number of telephone calls after he read the message. But he never phoned the one man he should have called: Marshall.

Roosevelt's instincts were correct. War was coming. It was a situation somewhat analogous to what Kimmel experienced on December 6, when he thought he should take his fleet to sea, but allowed himself to be talked out of the decision.

Roosevelt knew what the Japanese message meant, but instead of telling his subordinates that war was coming, getting them out of bed that night to work and find out what the next Japanese decrypts might say, Roosevelt demurred. He put everything on hold until a meeting could be convened the next morning at ten.

He didn't know the meeting, held in accordance with regular business hours, would be too late. He didn't know the Japanese were going to attack Pearl Harbor. He didn't know Kimmel and Short weren't ready to defend themselves.

Like the others who had access to Magic, Roosevelt thought he had time, when, in truth, time had run out.

The Commander in Chief of the Armed Forces failed to take prompt and effective action to bring his subordinates together to achieve a decision about what should be done. Thus, it is only fair that Roosevelt share the guilt with the other members of the military who have been named in this account.

Which gets me to another point.

One of the reasons to assign guilt to individuals for the disaster at Pearl Harbor is that the frailties of individuals and institutions are more understandable in such a context.

When I was a prosecutor, I never enjoyed winning a case and sending someone to jail. I felt sorry for the convict-to-be. I felt even sorrier for the members of his family, who suffered their loved one's perceived guilt even though they were innocent.

But by looking at the individuals and the deeds they did or did not commit as relates to Pearl Harbor, one comes to grips with the ultimate question: Did the system in which these people were embroiled work properly?

In the case of how Magic was handled before Pearl Harbor, the intelligence system, beset by human frailty, did not work.

President Roosevelt loved the Navy. He would never have allowed his precious ships and men to be sent to the bottom. That was not in his character. But Roosevelt favored the Navy over the Army. He chose the Navy over the Army to bring him the Magic decrypts. By so doing, he gave the Navy too much power in the intelligence field.

We're talking about a real-life situation, real human nature, not a sociology course. Roosevelt made a conscious decision to pat the Navy on the head, and the Navy turned around and bit him.

Thus, our President became the ultimate victim of Pearl Harbor.

If Commander Kramer had slept in his office the night of December 6, 1941, as hospital interns take catnaps while working hundred-hour weeks, then Roosevelt might have received that night the all-important fourteenth part of the diplomatic message, plus the following dispatch that came in between one and three A.M. December 7, saying it was to be handed to the American government at one P.M. Sunday. This would have given ample time to forestall the disaster that befell Pearl Harbor.

Before you, the reader, make up your own mind about the guilt or innocence of the people named [here], let me raise two final matters.

After Pearl Harbor, Kimmel and Short were relieved of command. They never again served on active duty. All the others named in this narrative, including those to whom I have assigned guilt, continued on active duty throughout the war. They served their nation well, many with true distinction. The fact that our judicial system allowed this continuing service to happen speaks well of it. The fact that we learned from Pearl Harbor, and created an independent National Security Agency to prevent similar disasters from occurring in the future, also speaks well of our democratic system of government.

The trick will be to ensure that our intelligence operations work properly in the future.

CHAPTER 2

Was the Internment of Japanese Americans Justified?

✴ Chapter Preface

Today, the consignment of Japanese Americans (or AJAs) to internment camps during World War II is well known and widely deplored. After the attack on Pearl Harbor in December 1941, many Americans living in western states worried that Americans of Japanese ancestry might have loyalties to Japan. Numerous government officials agreed. And on February 19, 1942, the president issued Executive Order 9066, authorizing the removal of AJAs from their homes and confinement in detention centers. A total of more than 120,000 people were interned in more than twenty camps, many until the war ended in 1945.

In the decades that followed, most Americans came to see that these actions were misguided, cruel, and a stain on the country's honor. As a result, several of the survivors have been compensated. Congress established the Commission on Wartime Relocation and Internment of Civilians (CWRIC) in 1980 to investigate the World War II detentions. CWRIC concluded that the cause had been "race prejudice, war hysteria, and a failure of political leadership" and recommended a payment of twenty thousand dollars to each internee. In 1988 CWRIC's recommendations became law, and in 1990 President George W. Bush apologized, saying in part, "A monetary sum and words alone cannot restore lost years or erase painful memories. . . . We can never fully right the wrongs of the past. But we can take a clear stand . . . and recognize that serious injustices were done."

Although nearly every American agrees that the wartime incarcerations were wrong and that the survivors deserve the government's apology, few people are aware of the significant contribution made by AJAs during the war. Some actually fought and died for the United States. And contrary to the initial fears of many Americans that Japanese Americans might betray the country, these troops distinguished themselves for bravery far beyond that demonstrated by the average American soldier.

When the attack on Pearl Harbor forced the United States into the war, approximately five thousand Nisei (AJAs born in America) were serving in the armed forces. Most of these men were summarily discharged due to fears that they would aid the enemy. However, in Hawaii the army allowed the formation in May 1942 of a combat unit made up of Nisei volunteers—the 100th Infantry Battalion. The unit was shipped first to North Africa (in June 1943) and then saw service in Italy. It became known as the "Purple Heart Battalion" because so many of its members received that medal for being wounded or killed.

In January 1943, the U.S. War Department formed a second unit of Nisei fighters—the 442nd Regimental Combat Team. This unit also distinguished itself in the European theater of the war. The combined Japanese American battalions became the most decorated U.S. military unit in the country's history (for their size and length of service). Their members received more than ninety-five hundred Purple Hearts and more than eighteen thousand decorations for bravery. Their achievements did much to deflate the controversy over the loyalty of AJAs in U.S. internment camps, showing that those who had argued for internment had acted in haste and out of unreasonable fear.

Viewpoint 1

"There is more potential danger among the group of Japanese who are born in this country than from the alien Japanese who were born in Japan."

Japanese Americans Constitute a Dangerous Security Threat

Earl Warren

Earl Warren is most famous for his service as chief justice of the U.S. Supreme Court from 1953 to 1969, during which he became renowned as a champion of civil rights. Ironically, however, back in 1942, only months after the devastating Japanese attack on Pearl Harbor, he was attorney general of California and a strong proponent of the idea that Japanese Americans posed a security threat to the country. The following essay is an excerpt from Warren's testimony to a congressional committee investigating security threats to the United States. He claims not only that Japanese Americans might collaborate with the enemy, but also that those who had been born in the United States (called Nisei) were even more likely to do so.

Earl Warren, testimony before the House Select Committee, Washington, DC, February 21 and 23, 1942.

For some time I have been of the opinion that the solution of our alien enemy problem with all its ramifications, which include the descendants of aliens, is not only a Federal problem but is a military problem. We believe that all of the decisions in that regard must be made by the military command that is charged with the security of this area. I am convinced that the fifth-column activities of our enemy call for the participation of people who are in fact American citizens, and that if we are to deal realistically with the problem we must realize that we will be obliged in time of stress to deal with subversive elements of our own citizenry.

If that be true, it creates almost an impossible situation for the civil authorities because the civil authorities cannot take protective measures against people of that character. We may suspect their loyalty. We may even have some evidence or, perhaps, substantial evidence of their disloyalty. But until we have the whole pattern of the enemy plan, until we are able to go into court and beyond the exclusion of a reasonable doubt establish the guilt of those elements among our American citizens, there is no way that civil government can cope with the situation.

On the other hand, we believe that in an area, such as in California, which has been designated as a combat zone, when things have happened such as have happened here on the coast, something should be done and done immediately. We believe that any delay in the adoption of the necessary protective measures is to invite disaster. It means that we, too, will have in California a Pearl Harbor incident.

I believe that up to the present and perhaps for a long time to come the greatest danger to continental United States is that from well organized sabotage and fifth-column activity.

"War Behind the Lines"?

California presents, perhaps, the most likely objective in the Nation for such activities. There are many reasons why that is true. First, the size and number of our naval and military establishments in California would make it attractive to our enemies as a field of sabotage. Our geographical position with relation to our enemy and to the war in the Pacific is also a tremendous factor. The number and the diversification of our war industries is extremely vital. The fire hazards due to our climate, our forest areas, and the type of building construction make us very susceptible to fire sabotage. Then the tremendous number of aliens that we have resident here makes it almost an impossible problem from the standpoint of law enforcement.

A wave of organized sabotage in California accompanied by an actual air raid or even by a prolonged black-out could not only be more destructive to life and property but could result in retarding the entire war effort of this Nation far more than the treacherous bombing of Pearl Harbor.

I hesitate to think what the result would be of the destruction of any of our big airplane factories in this State. It will interest you to know that some of our airplane factories in this State are entirely surrounded by Japanese land ownership or occupancy. It is a situation that is fraught with the greatest danger and under no circumstances should it ever be permitted to exist. . . .

In order to advise the committee more accurately on this subject I have asked the various district attorneys throughout the State to submit maps to me showing every Japanese ownership and occupancy in the State. Those maps tell a story, a story that is not very heartening to anyone who has the responsibility of protecting life and property either in time of peace or in war.

To assume that the enemy has not planned fifth column activities for us in a wave of sabotage is simply to live in a fool's paradise. These activities, whether you call them "fifth column activities" or "sabotage" or "war behind the lines upon civilians," or whatever you may call it, are just as much an integral part of Axis warfare as any of their military and naval operations. When I say that I refer to all of the Axis powers with which we are at war.

It has developed into a science and a technique that has been used most effectively against every nation with which the Axis powers are at war. It has been developed to a degree almost beyond the belief of our American citizens. That is one of the reasons it is so difficult for our people to become aroused and appreciate the danger of such activities. Those activities are now being used actively in the war in the Pacific, in every field of operations about which I have read. They have unquestionably, gentlemen, planned such activities for California. For us to believe to the contrary is just not realistic.

Unfortunately, however, many of our people and some of our authorities and, I am afraid, many of our people in other parts of the country are of the opinion that because we have had no sabotage and no fifth column activities in this State since the beginning of the war, that means that none have been planned for us. But I take the view that that is the most ominous sign in our whole situation. It convinces me more than perhaps any other factor that the sabotage that we are to get, the fifth column activities that we are to get, are timed just like Pearl Harbor was timed and just like the invasion of France, and of Denmark, and of Norway, and all of those other countries.

I believe that we are just being lulled into a false sense of security and that the only reason we haven't had disaster in California is because it has been timed for a different date, and that when that time comes if we don't do something about it it is going to mean disaster both to California and to our Nation. Our day of reckoning is bound to come in that regard. When, nobody knows, of course, but we are approaching an invisible deadline.

Following the attack on Pearl Harbor, Japanese Americans faced hostility and anti-Japanese sentiments from many Americans who viewed them as a security threat.

The Chairman [Rep. John H. Tolan]: On that point, when that came up in our committee hearings there was not a single case of sabotage reported on the Pacific coast, we heard the heads of the Navy and the Army, and they all tell us that the Pacific coast can be attacked. The sabotage would come coincident with that attack, would it not?

Attorney General Warren: Exactly.

The Chairman: They would be fools to tip their hands now, wouldn't they?

Attorney General Warren: Exactly. If there were sporadic sabotage at this time or if there had been for the last 2 months, the people of California or the Federal authorities would be on the alert to such an extent that they could not possibly have any real fifth column activities when the M-day comes. And I think that that should figure very largely in our conclusions on this subject.

Approaching an invisible deadline as we do, it seems to me that no time can be wasted in making the protective measures that are essential to the security of this State. And when I say "this State" I mean all of the coast, of course. I believe that Oregon and Washington are entitled to the same sort of consideration as the zone of danger as California. Perhaps our danger is intensified by the number of our industries and the number of our aliens, but it is much the same. . . .

The Younger Japanese Americans More of a Threat?

I want to say that the consensus of opinion among the law-enforcement officers of this State is that there is more potential danger among the group of Japanese who are born in this country than from the alien Japanese who were born in Japan. That might seem an anomaly to some people, but the fact is that, in the first place, there are twice as many of them. There are 33,000 aliens and there are 66,000 born in this country.

In the second place, most of the Japanese who were born in Japan are over 55 years of age. There has been practically no migration to this country since 1924. But in some instances the children of those people have been sent to Japan for their education, either in whole or in part, and while they are over there they are indoctrinated with the idea of Japanese imperialism. They receive their religious instruction which ties up their religion with their Emperor, and they come back here imbued with the ideas and the policies of Imperial Japan.

While I do not cast a reflection on every Japanese who is born in this country—of course we will have loyal ones—I do say that the consensus of opinion is that taking the groups by and large there is more potential danger to this State from the group that is born here than from the group that is born in Japan.

Mr. Arnold [Rep. Laurence F. Arnold]: Let me ask you a question at this point.

Attorney General Warren: Yes, Congressman.

Mr. Arnold: Do you have any way of knowing whether any one of this group that you mention is loyal to this country or loyal to Japan?

Attorney General Warren: Congressman, there is no way that we can establish that fact. We believe that when we are dealing with the Caucasian race we have methods that will test the loyalty of them, and we believe that we can, in dealing with the Germans and the Italians, arrive at some fairly sound conclusions because of our knowledge of the way they live in the community and have lived for many years. But when we deal with the Japanese we are in an entirely different field and we cannot form any opinion that we believe to be sound. Their method of living, their language, make for this difficulty. Many of them who show you a birth certificate stating that they were born in this State, perhaps, or born in Honolulu, can hardly speak the English language because, although they were born here, when they were 4 or 5 years of age they were sent over to Japan to be educated and they stayed over there through their adolescent period at least, and then they came back here thoroughly Japanese. . . .

I had together about 10 days ago about 40 district attorneys and about 40 sheriffs in the State to discuss this alien problem. I asked all of them collectively at that time if in their experience any Japanese, whether California-born or Japan-born, had ever given them any information on subversive activities or any disloyalty to this country. The answer was unanimously that no such information had ever been given to them.

Now, that is almost unbelievable. You see, when we deal with the German aliens, when we deal with the Italian aliens, we have many informants who are most anxious to help the local authorities and the State and Federal authorities to solve this alien problem. They come in voluntarily and give us information. We get none from the other source. . . .

Taking the Law into Their Own Hands

There is one thing that concerns us at the present time. As I say, we are very happy over the order of the President yesterday [Executive Order 9066]. We believe that is the thing that should be done, but that is only one-half of the problem, as we see it. It is one thing to take these people out of the area and it is another thing to do something with them after they get out. Even from the small areas that they have left up to the present time there are many, many Japanese who are now roaming around the State and roaming around the Western States in a condition that will unquestionably bring about race riots and prejudice and hysteria and excesses of all kind.

I hate to say it, but we have had some evidence of it in our State in just the last 2 or 3 days. People do not want these Japanese just loaded from one community to another, and as a practical matter it might be a very bad thing to do because we might just be transposing the danger from one place to another.

So it seems to me that the next thing the Government has to do is to find a way of handling these aliens who are removed from any vital zone.

In the county of Tulare at the present time and in the county of San Benito and in other counties there are large numbers of the Japanese moving in and sometimes the suggestion has come from the place that they leave, that they ought to go to this other community. But when they go there they find a hostile situation. We are very much afraid that it will cause trouble unless there is a very prompt solution of this problem.

My own belief concerning vigilantism is that the people do not engage in vigilante activities so long as they believe that their Government through its agencies is taking care of their most serious problem. But when they get the idea that their problems are not understood, when their Government is not doing for them the things that they believe should be done, they start taking the law into their own hands.

That is one reason why we are so happy that this committee is out here today because we believe that it will help us solve this problem quickly, which is just as important as to solve it permanently. . . .

Now, gentlemen, I have some maps which show the character of the Japanese land ownership and possessory interests in California. I will submit them at the time I submit a formal statement on the subject. These maps show to the law enforcement officers that it is more than just accident, that many of those ownerships are located where they are. We base that assumption not only upon the fact that they are located in certain places, but also on the time when the ownership was acquired.

It seems strange to us that airplane manufacturing plants should be entirely surrounded by Japanese land occupancies. It seems to us that it is more than circumstance that after certain Government air bases were established Japanese undertook farming operations in close proximity to them. You can hardly grow a jackrabbit in some of the places where they presume to be carrying on farming operations close to an Army bombing base.

Many of our vital facilities, and most of our highways are just pocketed by Japanese ownerships that could be of untold danger to us in time of stress.

So we believe, gentlemen, that it would be wise for the military to take every protective measure that it believes is necessary to protect this State and this Nation against the possible activities of these people.

Viewpoint 2

"We are Americans, not by the mere technicality of birth, but by all the other forces of sports, amusements, schools, churches, which are in our communities and which affect our lives directly."

Japanese Americans Do Not Pose a Security Threat

Michio Kunitani

In 1942 a special committee appointed by Congress held hearings in several western states to gather information and suggestions about the impending relocation of Japanese Americans. The committee was chaired by John H. Tolan of Oakland, California. Among those who testified before the committee were fifteen Japanese Americans, including Michio Kunitani, whose statement is reproduced here. Kunitani was an American-born citizen who had earlier voluntarily given up his Japanese citizenship and who represented a local political organization, the Nisei Democratic Club of Oakland. The main thrust of Kunitani's remarks is that Japanese Americans should not be treated any differently from Americans of German, Italian, or other descent.

Michio Kunitani, testimony before the House Select Committee, Washington, DC, February 21 and 23, 1942.

We come here as Americans prepared to take a frank attitude and make frank statements, and speak to the members of this committee here just as people probably would in the cloakroom of the House of Representatives. . . .

We come here as Americans, not by virtue of our birth in America, but by virtue of the social and cultural forces in America. We come here to be treated as Americans and we want to live as Americans in America.

As I say, we are Americans, not by the mere technicality of birth, but by all the other forces of sports, amusements, schools, churches, which are in our communities and which affect our lives directly.

Some of us are Yankee fans; some of us are Dodger fans; some like to sip beer; some like to go up to the Top of the Mark once in a while; we enjoy Jack Benny; we listen to Beethoven, and some of us even go through the Congressional Record. That is something.

The main idea that our group wanted to present here today was that we didn't want to be treated as a special group of enemy aliens and as descendants of enemy aliens. We want to be treated as Americans, or as other groups, such as Italians, Yugoslavs, or Finns.

It seems that among the reasons put forth by the committee, and the witnesses who testified this morning, and last Saturday, on why they thought that we should be treated as a special group were the following:

No. 1. Our physical characteristics.

No. 2. The question of dual citizenship.

No. 3. The vague question of Shintoism and national religion.

No. 4. The question of the language schools which many of us have attended.

Our group is in favor of evacuation if the military authorities of the United States deem it necessary. But if we do evacuate we think certain considerations should be taken into account:

No. 1. If we are evacuated we would like to have food, shelter, and clothing, whether it be in North Dakota, Arizona, or Florida.

No. 2. We think some plan should be instituted so that the evacuees can participate positively in the defense effort and that we can, by our efforts in some way help gain a quicker victory for the anti-Fascist forces.

No. 3. We want the evacuees who are in the various professions, such as doctors, opticians, lawyers, and so on, to continue to act in that capacity.

Are Japanese-Americans Loyal?

I would like to touch on the question of loyalty. There has been a hue and cry by a lot of the people in California that there has been no anti-Fascist action on the part of any Japanese group. I would like to refute that statement right here and now.

Our organization, since the Democratic campaign of 1938, has come out on numerous occasions against shipments of oil and scrap iron to the Fascist war lords of Japan, and we opposed aggression in Ethiopia. Our records are filled with communications to our Congressmen, even to our Representative, who happens to be Mr. Tolan, urging them to vote against such measures in Congress.

I want to touch upon the question of the language schools. I would like to point out to the members of the committee that our parents, most of them, have had very little education. You will find in any group, whether they be Jews, Yugoslavs, Finns, Danes, or Japanese, that the people who do migrate to other lands are usually those who have not had economic security in their native lands and, therefore, have come to new areas in order to gain a livelihood. Most of our parents fall into that category.

They set up these language schools for various reasons.

No. 1. They thought that since they enjoyed the fruits of American life that they should contribute something to America. They thought that the fine parts of Japanese culture could be integrated into American life and that the second generation of Japanese, if they were able to read and write, could thereby discover the better side of Japanese culture and they could give that as their contribution to America and, if they could do that, the parents would die happy.

No. 2. This so-called indoctrination on the part of our parents hasn't been only along Japanese lines, but it has also followed American lines. We had 500 students registered at the University of California last semester. That is the largest enrollment of any minority group in the State of California. The record will also show a large number of Japanese students attending universities and high schools.

There is another reason why a study of the Japanese language is encouraged and that is because a knowledge of the Japanese language is essential to the economic picture into which the Japanese man or woman has to fit. At least, in this generation most of our employers happen to be Japanese.

No Indoctrination

We were discriminated against in private industry and, therefore, the only other channel into which the Japanese people could gain an economic livelihood was in the Japanese group. It was essential for us to learn the Japanese language so that we could converse intelligently with our employers.

Another point that I want to bring out is that there aren't very many Japanese in the civil service of the Federal Government, or in the State and local governments. That those who are working for the Federal Government are in there because they are discriminated against in private industry. It is usually in the case of professional workers rather than, we will say, those who fall in the category of laborers.

Another point I want to bring out is that the time spent in language schools amounts to about an hour a day, maybe two or three times a week.

Most of the time of the Japanese student is spent in the public schools. He spends from 6 to 8 hours in public schools. After school he goes into the extra-curricular activity of the public schools. His Sundays and Saturdays are taken up by participation in athletic events, Boy Scout activities, and such.

The time element there is not present in which the young Japanese could be indoctrinated with Shintoism or anything else. . . .

Another point is this: Most of the second generation Japanese do not know the language sufficiently to be indoctrinated. In fact, most of our homes are places where, after dinner, we don't congregate around the living room, or at the dinner table and talk. Usually after 6 or 6:30 it is: "Well, I have to go to the basketball game," or "I have to go to a show."

That point is well brought out by the fact that the Army had to hire Japanese students to teach Japanese enrollees the Japanese language. That has been the case at Camp Roberts and at Fort Ord. It bears out my point that most of the Japanese, the young Japanese, don't know the language at all. . . .

The Question of Dual Citizenship

Now, I want to touch on the question of dual citizenship. I do not know very much about its history and background, but I can present my case in point.

I didn't even know that I was a citizen of Japan until I was about 17 years old, and a freshman in college. My father happened to tell me that I was a citizen of Japan. Therefore, I went through the legal channels and expatriated myself. . . .

Another thing I would like to point out to the members of the committee is the indivisibility of citizenship in the eyes of American law. If we are citizens here that is enough. I don't think all this cry about the question of dual citizenship is that important. I mean it doesn't play a major role in our lives.

Another thing in connection with dual citizenship that I would like to point out is that since the only other channel of expatriation has been closed to us by the closing of Japanese consulates, we favor the bill which was before Congress which provides that legal means be set up so that Japanese who have dual citizenship could expatriate themselves through American courts. Our organization is in favor of such a measure and we have written to our Congressman to support it.

Another thing I would like to point out, and it is probably a question you would ask me, is this: What about the recent raids by the F.B.I., when they found thousands of rounds of ammunition, sabers, binoculars, flashlights, and what not, in some of the homes, after the date set for turning in such contraband?

Our answer to that question is this: That our organization has instructed its members many times to tell their friends, and their parents, to surrender such things. I think most Japanese people have done this, and have carried out the regulation of the Department of Justice and the War Department in that connection.

Another thing I would like to point out is this: Which came first, the defense areas or the Japanese farms that are around the defense areas?

I would like to point out that agriculture was the first occupation open to the Japanese people. The people who came here first were agriculturalists. One-third of the present Japanese population in the United States is engaged in agricultural pursuits. It just happens that they have followed a pattern. It is a similar pattern in Des Moines, Iowa, in Jamestown, Va. as well as in California. It is a social pattern which is not peculiar to California, or to Washington. The fundamental basis is the same all over the United States. . . .

Another thing that I want to point out is that there is no conscious movement of Japanese to these areas. It is just simply a matter of following their occupations—farming. If it were third- or fourth-generation Japanese probably there might be—I mean if we found farms were around strategic areas, probably there would be a conscious effort by the Japanese to move around to certain areas, but I don't think at the present time, in this generation at least, there is any conscious movement on the part of the Japanese as a whole. . . .

Sabotage at Pearl Harbor?

Another point I want to bring out is about Pearl Harbor. We hear lots about sabotage at Pearl Harbor.

Mr. Tolan pointed out frequently this morning, and this afternoon, that he heard of Army trucks put in the road. I don't know where Mr. Tolan got that information. I don't know whether that is true or not. I cannot say. I can only go on the Roberts report, which was the only official United States document put out, as to what happened at Pearl Harbor, and why things happened as they did. I think if you gentlemen look into the Roberts report again you will find that no mention was made of sabotage on the part of Japanese-Americans. They pointed out that 200 members operating out of the Japanese consulate were the most active participants in fifth column activities in Hawaii.

I mean to say the average Japanese in California isn't intelligent enough to go about and engage in fifth column activities. The odds are against him. He has an oriental face that can be easily detected.

I am not saying there wasn't any fifth column activity in Pearl Harbor on the part of Japanese, but I don't think there was wholesale fifth column activity on the part of the Japanese-Americans or the aliens in Pearl Harbor. . . .

Another point I want to make is this idea of hardship cases. I think Congressman Tolan pointed out numerous times this morning what should be done about hardship cases.

Our organization has a definite plan as to what should be done about such cases if evacuation is to be instituted here in California.

No. 1. Our prime purpose is that we should not be treated any differently than Italians, Germans, Finns, or Yugoslavs. We want to be treated equally.

No. 2. We think that the Federal authorities should handle such cases. We don't believe that local authorities have the time, or the money, to set up agencies to take care of such cases.

We believe that the Federal Security Administration, under the able direction of Paul G. McNutt, should take the matter into its hands. I don't think the Army and Navy should do it. They have a big fight on their hands outside. I think they would be willing to let civilian bureaus handle this job of hardship cases. We think that the United States Employment Service, or the State social security board, should take such cases and deal with them.

I do not think any individual in America has any idea as to the numerous problems which will arise when you transplant a whole economy from one area to another. There are so many variables involved that I do not think anybody could begin to comprehend them.

Viewpoint 3

"Anti-Japanese sentiment was rooted in both racial and economic concerns."

The Internment of Japanese Americans Was Racist

Allan W. Austin

In this essay Allan W. Austin, who teaches history at Pennsylvania's College Misericordia, forcefully argues that the incarceration of thousands of Japanese Americans by the U.S. government during World War II was the result of nothing less than racism and ungrounded hysteria. He faults not only the government officials who issued the internment order, but also the press (especially in the western states) for its unwarranted incitement of the public, and the Supreme Court for not taking a stronger stand to protect American freedoms. Austin also makes the case that the general public was uneducated about Japanese culture, as well as the history and makeup of the Japanese American community, and therefore prone to believing claims by the press and government that Japanese Americans posed a threat.

Allan W. Austin, "Loyalty and Concentration Camps in America," *Last Witnesses: Reflections on the Wartime Internment of Japanese Americans*, edited by Erica Harth. New York: Palgrave, 2001. Copyright © 2001 by Erica Harth. All rights reserved. Reproduced by permission of St. Martin's Press, LLC.

Executive Order 9066[1] developed in the context of a long and often hysterical history of anti-Japanese agitation in the United States, especially in the Pacific coast states. Anti-Japanese sentiment was rooted in both racial and economic concerns and promoted by powerful local and national groups. Racism, fears generated by the upward economic mobility of Japanese Americans, and the external threat of Japanese militarism all provided preconditions for the government's decision to evacuate this population. Indeed, the strong antipathy created by anti-Japanese groups, especially through the promotion of the menacing idea of the "yellow peril," overran potential safeguards, such as an increasing concern for civil liberties, a liberal presidential administration, and the tradition of limited federal government action in the realm of internal security affairs, all of which might have militated against the decision for evacuation and relocation. The emotional anti-Japanese movement, which had previously proven its strength in shaping United States foreign policy and immigration law, would once again demonstrate its influence in the aftermath of the Japanese attack on the Pearl Harbor naval base on December 7, 1941.

In the months following Pearl Harbor, race became increasingly associated with loyalty in the United States. Despite the widely assumed relationship between race and disloyalty, the Federal Bureau of Investigation (FBI) originally arrested only 1,500 alien Japanese, although even this relative restraint resulted in the imprisonment of many who were clearly not a threat to national security. The rights of non-white Americans of enemy ancestry, it quickly became clear, were more likely to be violated in this early attempt at protecting the United States from internal subversion. As hostility grew, especially in the West Coast press, and came increasingly to focus on race and implied guilt, the American government began high-level talks concerning the possibility for mass incarceration.

An "Enemy Race"

General John L. DeWitt and the War Department almost immediately became the primary advocates of the mass evacuation and

---

1. Executive Order 9066, signed on February 19, 1942, allowed the U.S. Army to exclude "any and all persons" from vital "military areas."

incarceration of Japanese Americans. DeWitt, a jumpy commander prone to panic-ridden responses to even the most obvious false
alarms, was clearly a racist. The general referred to all Japanese as
members of an "enemy race" and explained to the already anxious
American public that "[a] Jap is a Jap. . . . It makes no difference
whether he is an American citizen, he is still Japanese." DeWitt
provided the first proposal for mass evacuation within seventy-two
hours of the Pearl Harbor attack and justified it with fantasies of a
looming Japanese American revolt. Major General Allen W. Gul-
lion, the provost Marshall general, supported calls for evacuation
by retreating from his earlier position that the military did not have
the authority to detain citizens as long as civilian courts were functioning, and he became willing to seize at least non-white civilians
without even a declaration of martial law. Although the cautious
DeWitt often shifted ground and seemed unwilling to commit to
any single policy recommendation, the War Department adopted
the goal of mass evacuation of Japanese Americans and began to
use its considerable wartime prestige and weight of opinion to
pressure the Department of Justice to exert more vigorous control
of this presumed potentially disloyal group.

Despite misgivings, the Justice Department eventually agreed to
the War Department's demands for a policy of mass incarceration.
Legal objections as well as Attorney General Francis Biddle's personal opposition to exile and incarceration were eventually pushed
aside in deference to the War Department's claims of "military necessity." The Justice Department's unwillingness to challenge the
military's definition of what was necessary for national security
and winning the war, in fact, seems to have been a key factor in its
decision to abdicate its important role in the formulation and implementation of internal security policy during the war. The War
Department's willingness to accept the administrative duties of
evacuation eliminated a final argument put forth by the Justice
Department against that policy. Popular civilian demands for a
vigorous program designed to ensure internal security may also
have helped to move the Justice Department to accede to the Department of War's demands. Other decision-makers were certainly aware of, and perhaps affected to some degree by, an
avalanche of mail that fit a discernible pattern of public opinion.

"Hello, you lousy Jap lover," began one not untypical letter to the apparently too-timid attorney general. "Why in hell don't you get out of office and let some one in there that's got guts. . . . You and your six freedoms should be put in the garbage can."

"Zero-Hour"?

The threat of Japanese American sabotage, espionage, and fifth column activities seemed to dominate popular concerns about Japanese Americans on the West Coast. Rumors of such actions, prevalent long before December 7, 1941, found broader circulation and increased legitimacy after alleged details of subversion related to the attack by the Japanese against Pearl Harbor became public knowledge. Indeed, many Americans seemed to connect alleged subversive activities—although none were ever proven—by Japanese Americans in Hawaii with the potential for danger in the West Coast states. Public statements by Earl Warren, the California attorney general, in the months after the Japanese attack on the American naval base in Hawaii both mirrored and reinforced this hysterical perspective. Warren argued that the West Coast represented the most likely Japanese target and ominously warned that the total lack of sabotage thus far provided convincing evidence of a concerted effort to hold back on all subversive activities until the well-planned-for "zero-hour" had arrived. Warren's testimony before the Tolan Committee reiterated these widely shared ideas: "To assume that the enemy has not planned fifth column activities for us in a wave of sabotage," he warned, "is simply to live in a fool's paradise." Such a coordinated attack, he contended, was inevitable. DeWitt's racist comments, because he was West Coast commander, lent verisimilitude to such warnings. Many accusers supported the general's position by pointing to "arrows" that had been constructed by traitorous Japanese Americans in a variety of ways, such as the strategic planting of flowers and tomato plants or stacking of hay, as clear evidence of plans to guide Japanese pilots to American defense plants and military bases. Warren added to this panic by suggesting that Japanese Americans congregated, quite intentionally, near defense plants, apparently ready to storm such plants after Japanese air raids. Daily newspaper reports of contraband seized from the Japanese

American community added to the hysteria. These perceptions resulted in increasing editorial support for the removal of the Japanese American population as well as the argument that evacuation was necessary to maintain public morale. Everybody would feel safer, the argument went, if all Japanese Americans were locked up in concentration camps.

The ties of Japanese Americans to Japan were often cited as proof of their disloyalty. That most adult Japanese Americans had supported Japan's military aggression in the 1930s was cited as proof of the Japanese American threat. Race obviously remained an implicit component of this argument. For example, the *Sacramento Bee* discussed only Japanese Americans, and not Americans of German or Italian descent, when it contended that "they cannot help but sympathize with their own country."

The Ultimate "Catch-22"

The institutions of Japanese Americans were also singled out as a subversive danger because of their close ties to the Japanese government—prefectural associations, language schools, and the Shinto and Buddhist religions were all identified as institutions that promoted an unbending allegiance to Japan. The flimsy evidence used to support these conclusions was accepted by a largely uninformed American public. The perverse logic of the times is shown by the argument that Japanese Americans clearly remained loyal to Japan because no Japanese American had ever informed on a subversive Japanese American.

Racism remained at the heart of most of the arguments designed to prove Japanese American disloyalty. Such feelings led to statements like "Once a Jap, always a Jap," and "You cannot regenerate a Jap, convert him, and make him the same person as a white man any more than you can reverse the laws of nature." Cultural considerations also played into the anti-Japanese hysteria that was seizing the American public. Japanese American culture simply made, some hypothesized, for an inferior Americanism. Education in the late-afternoon language schools fashioned students who were, for all intents and purposes, Japanese. Japanese religion also served as a deterrent to the development of 100 percent Americanism.

Burdened with such racial and cultural liabilities, Japanese Americans faced the ultimate "catch-22" when the federal government decided to send them into exile. Loyal Japanese Americans, many Americans argued, would willingly cooperate with all government decisions. Any who disobeyed were, by definition, disloyal. Thus, Japanese Americans who had acculturated politically and believed in the Constitution and the civil liberties that it was supposed to protect had to give up their freedom without protest. The alternative was clear: if one was not loyal enough to cooperate quickly with the government and move quietly to a concentration camp, one obviously belonged in such a camp as a disloyal person.

The War Relocation Authority (WRA), the civilian agency created on March 18, 1942, by Roosevelt's Executive Order 9102 to

As a response to public concern about sabotage, the U.S. government forced Japanese Americans into internment camps during World War II.

administer the concentration camps, quickly became aware that those camps bred frustrations, fear, and bitterness. Thus, by mid-1942, the WRA, fearing the permanent institutionalization of Japanese Americans, decided to initiate a process to release many of its prisoners. To do so without freeing disloyal and perhaps dangerous Japanese Americans, the WRA required a loyalty oath before release. This decision raised considerable controversy in the camps and resulted in 6,000 who refused to declare their loyalty to the United States and 3,000 who qualified their answer or chose not to answer (out of about 40,000 responses).

Morton Grodzins, a prominent early critic of the government's policy of evacuation, argues that various motives moved this substantial minority to answer no to the loyalty questions. Some did so to protest or to demand their rightful equal status. Others felt that loyalty to the nation meant disloyalty to the family. The fear of being removed from the camps and thrust back into what was perceived as a decidedly hostile environment led some to refuse to declare their loyalty. A final group answered no to express a preference for Japanese culture and to prepare for living in Japan. Living conditions, which varied considerably from camp to camp, also influenced decisions on this issue. The results of these loyalty questionnaires probably reinforced some attitudes about Japanese American disloyalty. However, Grodzins points out that "few, if any, would ever have openly declared themselves not loyal to the United States [if not faced with a forced, direct choice]."

"A Pervasive Racism"

Executive Order 9066 was almost immediately endorsed by Congress and, in 1943 and 1944, by the Supreme Court. Congress accepted the War Department's claim of "military necessity" without question, never pausing to examine critically the situation and the issues involved. What little study Congress undertook has been described by Grodzins as full of "misunderstanding and irrelevancy." The Supreme Court's approval relaxed its standards for civil liberties. In the *Hirabayashi* decision in June 1943, the court, grounding its racist decision in the prevailing popular conception of racial guilt, upheld the legitimacy of emergency curfew regulations that affected only ethnic Japanese, aliens and citizens alike. The Supreme Court would not rule again on the constitutionality of the government's actions until December 1944. In *Korematsu*, a no-longer-unanimous court sustained, in effect, the legality of the forced exile of citizens of Japanese ancestry. The serious dangers of 1942, the court continued to maintain, justified these policy decisions. The *Endo* decision was handed down on the same day as *Korematsu*. While *Endo* did assert that loyal citizens could not continue to be held in concentration camps, the case did not result in a repudiation of the evacuation. The Supreme Court faulted only the administrative processes of the WRA, not the decision to implement a program of exile and incarceration, in its ruling.

Grodzins argued soon after the war that the national government had succeeded in one of its main tasks, winning the war, but had failed in an equally important task, protecting democracy at home. He argued that American policies toward the Japanese American population had been the antithesis of democracy, more closely resembling the directions one might find in "the totalitarian handbook." Japanese Americans, he continued, had been victimized by a pervasive racism as well as by economic and political goals that had become intertwined with and ultimately inseparable from the issue of patriotism. The arguments for evacuation reflected these mixed motives but seemed to focus on the underlying issue of race and disloyalty.

The exile and incarceration of Japanese Americans during the Second World War was not an action entirely without precedent in American history. . . . The reservations established for Native Americans were precursors of the Second World War's concentration camps. However, the government's concentration camp program for the Second World War was unprecedented as an act of mass incarceration of American citizens. The wartime camps, furthermore, were built with a very specific and unprecedented purpose: to house a group of people assumed to be guilty of disloyalty solely on the basis of ancestry. Indeed, considerations of race, and not individual actions, drove this determination of guilt.

Although the decision of mid-February 1942 to incarcerate Japanese Americans on the mainland faced little initial opposition, a growing number of critics began to question both the mer-

its and the future implications of this policy as the war progressed.
. . . Morton Grodzins noted the potential future ramifications of
the Japanese American incarceration as early as 1949, warning that
wartime actions against this group could be repeated against other
unpopular minority groups: "The process of government is a continuing process; what it produced for Japanese Americans it can
also produce for other Americans."

Viewpoint 4

"Americans have nothing to be ashamed of about this episode, even though it is regrettable that war and its incidents ever have to happen."

The Internment of Japanese Americans Was Not Racist

Dwight D. Murphey

In this article Dwight D. Murphey, an attorney and associate editor of the *Conservative Review*, contends that leftist political advocates tend to be too critical of the United States and its foreign policy. As an example, he points to the current popular view that the internment of Japanese Americans during World War II was motivated by racism and revealed deep-seated racism in American society. First, says Murphey, the so-called internment might better be termed a relocation, since not all of the Japanese Americans involved lived inside the camps. Second, he makes the case that fears that some Japanese Americans might collaborate with the enemy were well founded and not motivated by racism.

Dwight D. Murphey, "The World War II Relocation of Japanese-Americans," *Journal of Social, Political, and Economic Studies*, Spring 1993. Copyright © 1993 by Dwight D. Murphey. Reproduced by permission.

Many aspects of American life and history have come under attack by those who feel a deep alienation against the mainstream of American society. This hostile critique has been especially intense since the 1960s, but reflects a long-term phenomenon which has been one of the main facts about the United States since as long ago as the 1820s: the "alienation of the intellectual." The American people are not above criticism. It would be foolish to defend them categorically with regard to everything that has happened over their long history. And yet, I am persuaded that they are not and have not been, as a people, "befouled," as the critics from the Left have long wished us to believe.

Several issues have been most salient as part of the Left's attack. As to them, the existing literature is overwhelmingly one-sided, presenting a hostile critique. Is there "another side"?

In . . . essays that I wrote for the *Journal of Social, Political and Economic Studies* and the *Conservative Review* in the early 1990s, I approached each of these issues with a simple question: "What would a scholar, seeking to be thorough and objective, and yet at the same time not bringing to the subject a deep animus against the United States, think about what happened?". . .

When I started my study of the removal of the Japanese-Americans I knew virtually nothing about it, and I have remained ready to report whatever I found. It obviously should not be a disqualification, though, for a scholar to begin his study of any of these issues without a prior animus against the United States.

Nor should proving the scholar's "objectivity" require him to find reason for America to be ashamed when that isn't called for. In my opinion, the United States did *not* act shamefully in its treatment of persons of Japanese ancestry during World War II. In fact, a better case could be made for a diametrically opposite criticism: that the treatment was so tender-hearted that it actually endangered the security of the United States during a desperate war.

In the intolerant context of today's ideological arguments, it is predictable that a conclusion favorable to the United States will be represented as "offensive" to the many splendid people of Japanese ancestry who now form a part of the American people. But that, of course, is nonsense. The search for historical accuracy isn't a panderer's game to curry favor. To seek the truth is no slander against anyone. . . .

There is so much to the subject that will be helpful for me to start, like a debater, by "telling you what I am going to tell you." Most of what follows will relate to two large questions:

• First, what exactly was done regarding the persons of Japanese ancestry?

• Second, why was it done?; i.e., what was its necessity?. . .

The West Coast a Military Zone

Immediate arrest of "dangerous aliens" after Pearl Harbor. Within days after the December 7, 1941, Japanese attack on Pearl Harbor, approximately 3,000 Japanese aliens classified as dangerous were arrested and incarcerated by the Department of Justice. These were individuals under suspicion by American intelligence agencies, which beginning in 1939 had begun to compile lists of persons considered dangerous in case of war. (This group was included among those who received an apology and $20,000 each in the early 1990s for "mental suffering.")

Declaration of the West Coast as a military zone; exclusion of persons of Japanese origin. On February 19, 1942, President Franklin D. Roosevelt signed Executive Order 9066. This authorized the establishment of military areas from which people of all kinds could be excluded. Lt. General John L. DeWitt was appointed the military commander to carry out the Executive Order. In March, Gen. DeWitt declared large parts of the Pacific Coast states military areas in which no one of Japanese descent would be allowed to remain. The exclusion order affected Japanese-Americans living on the West Coast by forcing them to move inland. Its only effect upon those who already lived inland was to bar them from going to the quarantined areas on the West Coast.

Col. Karl R. Bendetsen was named Director of the Wartime Civil Control Administration to handle the evacuation. Also in March, Roosevelt created a civilian agency, the War Relocation Authority (WRA), to assist the evacuees. Milton Eisenhower, brother of later president Dwight Eisenhower, was named Director. Congress ratified the evacuation by enacting legislation that made it a federal offense for anyone to violate the exclusion order.

A short-lived plan originally was to assist the Japanese-

Americans in a process by which they would move inland "on their own recognizance" as individuals and families. Bendetsen [in 1981 testimony before the Commission on Wartime Relocation and Internment of Civilians] says that "funds were provided for them [and] we informed them . . . where there were safe motels in which they could stay overnight." This was ended almost immediately, by late March, however; Bendetsen says that the need for a more organized system became apparent when most of the Japanese-Americans were not able to make arrangements to relocate quickly even with some help. A second reason was that the governors of western states (reflecting public opinion in their states) objected strongly to thousands of people of Japanese origin moving into their states without oversight. These objections were reiterated at a Governors' Conference for ten western governors on April 7. (There was a continuing tension, lessening over time, between the desire to let the evacuees relocate freely and the public's desire to have them closely monitored.)

The Relocation Centers

This led to the "assembly center phase," during which the evacuees were moved to improvised centers such as race tracks and fairgrounds along the West Coast pending the construction of ten "relocation centers" in eastern California, Arizona, Utah, Idaho, Wyoming, Colorado, and as far east as Arkansas. During this phase, federal officials made extensive efforts to lessen public hostility. As those feelings subsided, approximately 4,000 families moved inland "on their own recognizance" to communities of their choice before the assembly center phase was over at the end of the summer of 1942. Bendetsen says that all of the Japanese-Americans could have moved on their own at any time if they had seen their way clear to do it.

The assembly centers are criticized as having had "barbed wire and searchlights," overcrowding, lack of privacy, and inadequate medical care. But Bendetsen disputes virtually all of this, as we will see in my later discussion of whether the evacuees can properly be said to have been "interned." Hastily improvised and purely temporary quarters for thousands of people who have been uprooted from their homes on short notice could not have been pleasant.

There is no incongruity, however, between this and the fact, also true, that the government worked with the evacuees to take extraordinary measures to make the centers as comfortable as possible. In the short time they existed, some centers opened libraries; movies were shown regularly; there were Scout troops, arts and crafts classes, musical groups, and leagues for basketball and baseball. Three hundred and fifty people signed up for a calisthenics class at Stockton. All had playgrounds for children, and one even had a pitch-and-putt golf course. The centers were run almost entirely by the Japanese-Americans themselves.

As the ten relocation centers became ready, the evacuees were moved to them from the assembly centers. These were under the jurisdiction of the War Relocation Authority. Dillon S. Myer became the Director of the WRA in June when Milton Eisenhower resigned to become the deputy director of the Office of War Information. The relocation centers' highest population, of 106,770, was attained on November 1, 1942. The construction of the camps was of the type used for housing American soldiers overseas—which is to say, the centers were austere but functional. Senator S. I. Hayakawa later described them [in *Through the Communication Barrier*, 1979] as "dreary places: long rows of tarpaper-covered wooden barracks. . . . Each room had a stove, a drop light, an iron cot and mattress. . . . But the WRA," he said, "headed by the wise and humane Dillon Myer, . . . made life as comfortable as possible for them." It is worth noting that no families were ever separated during the process. . . .

Tule Lake Center used for actual internment. The center at Tule Lake, California, started as a relocation center but was soon turned into an actual internment camp—a "segregation center"—for those Japanese-Americans who were hostile to the United States. It housed those who applied to be repatriated to Japan if they had not withdrawn the application by the middle of 1943; those who answered "no" to a loyalty questionnaire and didn't clear up the problem in special hearings held for the purpose; those against whom the government had evidence of disloyalty; and the family members of those in the first three groups. . . .

Were the relocation centers an "internment"? There is no question but that the evacuees were forced by law to leave their homes on the West Coast and to either stay in the centers or relocate elsewhere in the United States by receiving leaves for the purpose. Their exclusion from the West Coast was not voluntary, and after the short-lived initial phase their relocation had to be done through the centers, which granted leave, temporary or indefinite, for the purpose. But, except for those arrested as "dangerous aliens" right after Pearl Harbor and those who were later segregated at Tule Lake, were the Japanese-Americans "interned" in the centers? And were the centers, as is often charged, "concentration camps"?

It is important to realize that these questions are largely issues of characterization. Those who want to place the evacuation in the worst light stress the "humiliation" and "affront to our loyalty" inherent in being made to relocate. They especially like to speak of the centers as "concentration camps," thereby evoking images of the horrors of Nazi concentration camps. . . .

The substance of the charge of "internment" is contradicted by the fact that resettlement outside the centers was diligently pursued throughout the process. Hayakawa says that by January 2, 1945, half of those evacuated had "found new jobs and homes in mid-America and the East." What is most often pointed to in support of the charge of "internment" and even of the centers' being "concentration camps" is that there were "fences and guards." Even Hayakawa speaks of the centers as being "behind barbed wire, guarded by armed sentries." Oddly, however, the role of fences and guards depends largely upon perception. . . .

The Danger Is Real

The nature of the military emergency. A situation of extreme military vulnerability existed in December 1941 and early 1942. The American Pacific Fleet, the United States' first line of defense in the Pacific, was destroyed by the December 7 Japanese attack on Pearl Harbor. The Japanese at the same time attacked Hong Kong, Malaysia, the Philippines, Wake and Midway Islands. The next day, they invaded Thailand. Within less than a week, Guam fell. By Christmas they had taken Wake Island and had occupied Hong Kong. Manila fell on January 2, and Singapore on February 10. The Battle of the Java Sea on February 27 resulted in a major Japanese naval victory. By early March Japan had control over

Rangoon, Burma and the Netherlands East Indies. The struggle at Bataan and Corregidor marked the end of the Japanese conquest of the Philippines. The Hawaiian Islands and the West Coast of the United States were unprotected from attack. On February 23 a Japanese submarine shelled an oil field along the California coast. Two days later five unidentified planes were spotted and Los Angeles underwent a black-out. The United States hurriedly made preparations for war. The extent of its unpreparedness is graphically illustrated by the draftees' use of wooden guns in their maneuvers in Louisiana in early 1942.

Japanese exploitation of West Coast vulnerability. The critics of the evacuation often argue that there was no demonstrated military necessity for it. The [1982] Report of the Commission on Wartime Relocation [a presidential commission appointed to investigate U.S. relocation policy] speaks of "the clamor" by California officials for protective action, and says that "these opinions were not informed by any knowledge of actual military risks." The

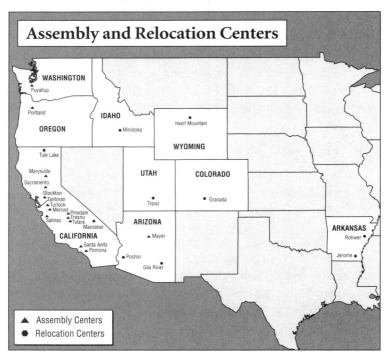

Assembly and Relocation Centers

extensive critical literature mocks the perception of danger, suggesting that it was a figment of hysterical imaginations.

But this is nonsense. The danger was apparent to anyone who considered the situation. Earl Warren, as attorney general of California, testified before a select committee of Congress (the "Tolan Committee") on February 21, 1942, and submitted letters from a number of local officials. Some pointed to the vulnerability of the water supply and of the large-scale irrigation systems: "It would be absolutely humanly impossible," one of them wrote, "for the small force now available in the sheriff's office to make even a pretense of guarding this tremendous farm territory and the irrigation system." Another pointed out that "a systematic campaign of incendiarism would cause terrific disaster" during the California dry season from May until October. The city manager of Alameda observed that "we have the naval air station at one end of the island. . . . There are five major shipyards along the northern edge and there is the Oakland Airport at the eastern end of the island." Warren provided maps that showed that the Japanese-American population lived in close proximity to virtually all strategic locations.

Many scenarios suggest themselves. Espionage, sabotage and aid to an invading army are obvious possibilities. To appreciate the danger we need a very real sense of what a terrible toll could have been exacted if even another Pearl Harbor had been committed. The potential, however, was for much more than that.

In addition to the civilian population, there was much that was important militarily and economically along the West Coast; it was clearly exposed; and there were few means to defend it. This was enough in itself to create a critical emergency, to be met as humanely but as effectively as possible. It should not be necessary for the American government to have known specifically of plans for espionage and sabotage.

Just the same, there *was* definitive evidence of Japan's intent to exploit (and actual exploitation of) the situation. On December 4, 1941, the Office of Naval Intelligence reported a Japanese "intelligence machine geared for war, in operation, and utilizing west coast Japanese." On January 21, 1942, a bulletin from Army Intelligence "stated flat out that the Japanese government's espionage net containing Japanese aliens, first and second generation Japanese and other nationals is now thoroughly organized and working underground," according to the [1984 congressional] testimony of David D. Lowman, a retired career intelligence officer who has written extensively on declassified intelligence from World War II.

Worries About Spies

The Commission on Wartime Relocation contradicted this in its 1982 Report when it said that "not a single documented act of espionage, sabotage or fifth column activity was committed by an American citizen of Japanese ancestry or by a resident Japanese alien on the West Coast." This claim is often repeated in the critical literature, but is blatantly false.

Amazingly, the Commission ignored the most important source of information about espionage, which is the dispatches sent by the Japanese government to its own officials before and during the war. U.S. Navy codebreakers had broken the Japanese diplomatic code in 1938, and the decoded messages were distributed, on a basis "higher than Top Secret," to a small handful of the very highest American officials under the codename "MAGIC." Lowman testified in 1984 that "included among the diplomatic communications were hundreds of reports dealing with espionage activities in the United States and its possessions. . . . In recruiting Japanese second generation and resident nationals, Tokyo warned to use the utmost caution. . . . In April [1941], Tokyo instructed all the consulates to wire home lists of first- and second-generation Japanese according to specified categories." The result, he said, was that "in May 1941, Japanese consulates on the west coast reported to Tokyo that first and second generation Japanese had been successfully recruited and were now spying on shipments of airplanes and war material in the San Diego and San Pedro areas. They were reporting on activities within aircraft plants in Seattle and Los Angeles. Local Japanese . . . were reporting on shipping activities at the Bremerton Naval Yard. . . . The Los Angeles consulate reported: 'We shall maintain connections with our second generation who are at present in the Army to keep us informed' . . . Seattle followed with a similar dispatch."

Several officials within the Roosevelt administration opposed the evacuation of the Japanese-Americans from the West Coast, but Lowman makes a telling point: that the President, the Secretary of War, the Army Chief of Staff, the Director of Military Intelligence, the Secretary of the Navy, the Chief of Naval Operations, the Director of Naval Intelligence, and the Chiefs of Army and Navy Plans—all of whom received MAGIC—*favored* evacuation. It was those who did not have knowledge of the Japanese dispatches who found it possible, somewhat incongruously in light of the self-evident factors I have mentioned, to doubt the military necessity.

Critics who damn the United States for the evacuation have sought to minimize the significance of MAGIC. John J. McCloy, who was Assistant Secretary of War during the war, testified in 1984 that "word has gone out now from the lobbyists to 'laugh off' the revelations of MAGIC."

The Commission on Wartime Relocation, established by Congress in 1980 and composed of such prominent figures as Arthur E. Goldberg, Arthur S. Flemming, Senator Edward Brooke, and Robert F. Drinan, didn't bother to laugh MAGIC off—it simply ignored it. . . .

The unassimilated nature of the Japanese-American community. The nature of the Japanese-American community on the West Coast at the time of World War II posed a dual problem. Because it was tightly-knit and unassimilated, it was attractive to Japan as a field for cultivation. At the same time, it was virtually impenetrable to efforts of the American government to sort out those whose loyalties were with Japan. . . .

The critics blame American caucasians for this lack of assimilation, pointing to the hostility that had been shown toward Asian immigrants by labor unions and others on the West Coast during the preceding decades. That, though, is another issue, one that asks whether it is wrong for the citizens of a country to oppose large-scale immigration by people who are considerably different from themselves. What is relevant to the question of the military emergency during World War II is not who was at fault for the Japanese-American community's lack of assimilation, but the uncontradicted fact that they were not assimilated. . . .

Were Japanese-Americans Loyal?

How loyal were the Japanese-Americans? This brings us to the most sensitive part of the study, since the "politically correct" thing to say is that *all* of the second-generation Japanese-Americans (the Nisei, who were the first to be born here, and even the Kibei, who were sent back to Japan for their education) were pro-American. I have already referred to Senator Hayakawa's sweeping generalization, which is bound to be appealing: "They had grown up loyal Americans." Accordingly, it is important to note again that it is no reflection on today's Americans of Japanese ancestry to take an honest look at what the situation was fifty years ago during World War II.

Many did strongly identify with the American side, and even distinguished themselves in combat on behalf of this country. An all-Nisei National Guard unit from Hawaii, the 100th Battalion, fought in Italy, winning much distinction, and was later merged into a newly-formed group, the 442nd [Regimental] Combat Team, which went on to fight in both Italy and France. . . .

To focus exclusively on this, however, obscures the truth, which taken as a whole was much more complex. Here are some aspects of that complexity:

• The War Relocation Authority had the evacuees fill out a questionnaire about their loyalty. Colonel Frederick Wiener testified [before Congress] in 1984 that "they asked first of the persons of military age whether they would serve in the Armed Forces of the United States; 94 percent of them gave negative answers. Now I will admit that it is asking a great deal of an individual after he is interned as a security risk [sic] to volunteer cheerfully for service. . . . I do not criticize it. What I criticize is that the 94 percent who didn't serve now wrap themselves in the regimental colors of the 442d RCT."

• A significant number sought repatriation to Japan. 9,028 applications were filed by the end of 1943, a total that swelled to 19,014 by a year later. Eventually, more than 16 percent of the evacuees asked for repatriation. Of these, 8,000 actually went back to Japan. In 1982 the Congressional Commission put the most favorable spin on this by blaming it on the evacuation: "No other statistics chronicle so clearly as these the decline of evacuees' faith in the United States." In any case, it runs clearly counter to the example set by those who served in the 442nd Combat Team.

• There was a powerful pro-Japan element within the relocation centers, forcing its members' eventual segregation into the facility at Tule Lake. Secretary of War Henry L. Stimson wrote in May 1943 about "a vicious, well-organized, pro-Japanese group to be found at each relocation center. Through agitation and violence, these groups gained control of many aspects of internal project administration, so much so that it became disadvantageous, and sometimes dangerous, to express loyalty to the United States." In the fall of 1942 some of the leaders of the Japanese American Citizens League were beaten by gangs after passing a resolution supporting the United States. Sometimes the pro-Japan element formed a competing system of center governance, electing its own block representatives. At the Manzanar center, a group called the Black Dragons championed Japan. . . .

• If Japan had invaded the West Coast, enormous pressures would have come to bear to support the invading army. Col. Bendetsen testified that wherever the Japanese invaded they shot those of Japanese ancestry who did not embrace them—and that this fact was well known. . . .

No Need to Invoke Racism

Why wasn't the same done with the Hawaiian Japanese-Americans? The point is sometimes made that the evacuation from the West Coast was inconsistent with having left the Japanese-American population on Hawaii. The answer is that with the declaration of martial law and the suspension of the writ of habeas corpus in December 1941, Hawaii was placed under direct military control. . . . This was not done on the mainland.

Why weren't Americans of German and Italian extraction evacuated? Another point of criticism asks why the Japanese-Americans were evacuated but people of German and Italian ancestry were not. This has a double edge: it suggests that the evacuation really wasn't necessary; and it suggests that the evacuation was racially motivated.

Senator Hayakawa wrote that "the answer is obvious. Germans and Italians, having come to America earlier than the Japanese and in far greater numbers, were already well-known to Americans in 1941." The same point was expressed in a letter that the city officials of Madera, California, wrote to then–attorney general Earl Warren in early 1942: "The general feeling about the Italians is that they are well assimilated, and we do not regard even the Italian aliens alien in fact. . . . So far as we know, there are no German aliens in this community." The distinction lies in the vast difference in assimilation. The Germans and Italians had longsince become mixed with the general population. . . .

Was the relocation a product of "racism"? Much public opinion on the West Coast had long been hostile to Japanese and other Asian immigration. Organized labor was for many years prominent among its opponents. And there is no question but that public opinion was inflamed against the Japanese during World War II, especially immediately following Pearl Harbor. This feeling was most intense on the West Coast, for a very specific reason: the National Guard units from eleven western states were fighting in the Philippines, where they were tortured and starved by their Japanese captors. Their families and friends felt passionately about these atrocities.

Throughout the war, one of the motivating factors in the policy of evacuation and resettlement was to protect the Japanese-Americans from public anger. It is easy today to say that that anger was "racist," but we have reason to be suspicious of attitudes taken under much more comfortable circumstances forty and even fifty years after the fact. To argue that the anger was vicious has, itself, a certain vicious quality about it.

There were ample reasons for the evacuation that had nothing to do with racism. Justice Hugo Black wrote level-headedly about this in 1944 [*Korematsu v. United States*]: "To cast this case into outlines of racial prejudice, without reference to the real military dangers which were present, merely confuses the issue. Korematsu was not excluded from the Military Area because of hostility to him or his race. . . . He *was* excluded because we are at war with the Japanese Empire.". . .

The circumstances during World War II were much more complicated than those who would damn the United States as having "viciously set up concentration camps for the Japanese-Americans" ever admit. My study of the subject has persuaded me that Americans have nothing to be ashamed of about this episode, even though it is regrettable that war and its incidents ever have to happen. We should, however, be ashamed of the way in which we as a people have wallowed in self-abasement in our eagerness to be "generous" and "sensitive" in response to the bitter censures of alienated ideology. Most Americans I have talked with are thoroughly uninformed as to what actually happened and why, and yet are eager to join in the condemnation of the actions of the United States.

CHAPTER 3

Was Dropping the Atomic Bomb Necessary?

✵ Chapter Preface

One of the most important and far-reaching decisions made by American leaders during World War II was to develop and use the atomic bomb on Japanese cities. Even after six decades, debate still rages in some quarters over whether employing the bomb was necessary. Much of the controversy surrounding this weapon of mass destruction undoubtedly derives from the fact that its use could not be concealed and that it killed many thousands of people, a large proportion of them civilians.

In reviewing the arguments for and against the use of the atomic bomb more than half a century after the fact, it is revealing that a number of the scientists who helped build the bomb did not feel it should ever be deployed. In the months leading up to the destruction of Hiroshima on August 6, 1945, two panels of American scientists met to prepare recommendations to the White House. The main question considered by each panel was whether it would be feasible and/or ultimately effective to give the Japanese a demonstration of the weapon's power. If Japan's leaders saw an atomic bomb detonated in an uninhabited area, would they be sufficiently impressed and frightened to surrender and end the war?

One panel of scientists, which met in Los Alamos, New Mexico, in early June, concluded that a demonstration would not be realistic. In their view, exploding a bomb in a remote region might be misleading. Japanese leaders might assume that most of the people in a targeted city could find sufficient cover to avoid the effects of the blast. Thus, the panel issued a report that said in part: "We can propose no technical demonstration likely to bring an end to the war. We can see no acceptable alternative to direct military use."

In contrast, the other panel, chaired by German-born scientist James Franck, concluded the opposite. The members were concerned not only about the unnecessary killing of thousands of Japanese civilians by the bomb. They also feared that using the weapon on cities would lead to other nations striving to get the bomb. The United States would then be susceptible to attack by weapons of mass destruction invented by its own people. The panel's report to the White House read in part:

> If the United States were to be the first to [use the bomb, it]
> would precipitate the race for armaments and prejudice the
> possibility of reaching an international agreement on the fu-
> ture control of such weapons. Much more favorable condi-
> tions for the eventual achievement of such an agreement
> could be created if nuclear bombs were first revealed to the
> world by a demonstration in an appropriately selected unin-
> habited area.

President Harry S Truman and his advisers weighed these reports along with other data and concluded that it was necessary
to drop the bomb on Japanese cities. This action did bring the war
to an end. But this outcome does not rule out the possibility that
the demonstration recommended by Franck's panel would have
been equally effective. At the least, it can be argued that part of
what Franck and his colleagues said about the use of nuclear
weapons—that they would become part of an international arms
race—turned out to be right. Following the war, a Cold War nuclear standoff ensued between the United States and the Soviet
Union, which lasted until the late 1980s. Meanwhile, several other
nations sought to acquire such weapons and join the growing
"nuclear club."

Viewpoint 1

"The reasons which underlay our use of [the atomic bomb against Japan] . . . have always seemed compelling and clear, and I cannot see how any person vested with such responsibilities as mine could have taken any other course."

Dropping the Atomic Bomb Was Justified

Henry L. Stimson

President Roosevelt appointed Henry L. Stimson as secretary of war (a position now called secretary of defense) in 1940, and Stimson continued in that post under Roosevelt's successor, Harry Truman. Stimson was therefore directly involved in the momentous decision made in 1945 to drop atomic bombs on Japan. After conferring in private with a number of leading scientists and military officials, Stimson recommended the use of these weapons to Truman, who soon afterward ordered their deployment. This essay is a reprint of a magazine article penned by Stimson shortly after the war, in which he defended his and Truman's decision.

In recent months there has been much comment about the decision to use atomic bombs in attacks on the Japanese cities of

Henry L. Stimson, "The Decision to Use the Atomic Bomb," *Harper's Magazine,* February 1947, pp. 120–27. Copyright © 1947, renewed in 1974 by Harper's Magazine Foundation. All rights reserved. Reproduced by permission.

Hiroshima and Nagasaki. This decision was one of the gravest made by our government in recent years, and it is entirely proper that it should be widely discussed. I have therefore decided to record for all who may be interested my understanding of the events which led up to the attack on Hiroshima on August 6, 1945, on Nagasaki on August 9, and the Japanese decision to surrender, on August 10. No single individual can hope to know exactly what took place in the minds of all of those who had a share in these events, but what follows is an exact description of our thoughts and actions as I find them in the records and in my clear recollection.

It was in the fall of 1941 that the question of atomic energy was first brought directly to my attention. At that time President Roosevelt appointed a committee consisting of Vice President [Henry] Wallace, General [George C.] Marshall, Dr. Vannevar Bush, Dr. James B. Conant, and myself. The function of this committee was to advise the President on questions of policy relating to the study of nuclear fission which was then proceeding both in this country and in Great Britain. For nearly four years thereafter I was directly connected with all major decisions of policy on the development and use of atomic energy, and from May 1, 1943, until my resignation as Secretary of War on September 21, 1945, I was directly responsible to the President for the administration of the entire undertaking; my chief advisers in this period were General Marshall, Dr. Bush, Dr. Conant, and Major General Leslie R. Groves, the officer in charge of the project. At the same time I was the President's senior adviser on the military employment of atomic energy. . . .

In the spring of 1945 it became evident that the climax of our prolonged atomic effort was at hand. By the nature of atomic chain reactions, it was impossible to state with certainty that we had succeeded until a bomb had actually exploded in a fullscale experiment; nevertheless it was considered exceedingly probable that we should by midsummer have successfully detonated the first atomic bomb. This was to be done at the Alamogordo Reservation in New Mexico. It was thus time for detailed consideration of our future plans. What had begun as a well-founded hope was now developing into a reality. . . .

The Opinions of the Experts

The Interim Committee was charged with the function of advising the President on the various questions raised by our apparently imminent success in developing an atomic weapon. I was its chairman, but the principal labor of guiding its extended deliberations fell to George L. Harrison, who acted as chairman in my absence. It will be useful to consider the work of the committee in some detail. . . .

The discussions of the committee ranged over the whole field of atomic energy, in its political, military, and scientific aspects. That part of its work which particularly concerns us here relates to its recommendations for the use of atomic energy against Japan, but it should be borne in mind that these recommendations were not made in a vacuum. The committee's work included the drafting of the statements which were published immediately after the first bombs were dropped, the drafting of a bill for the domestic control of atomic energy, and recommendations looking toward the international control of atomic energy. The Interim Committee was assisted in its work by a Scientific Panel whose members were the following: Dr. A.H. Compton, Dr. Enrico Fermi, Dr. E.O. Lawrence, and Dr. J.R. Oppenheimer. All four were nuclear physicists of the first rank; all four had held positions of great importance in the atomic project from its inception. At a meeting with the Interim Committee and the Scientific Panel on May 31, 1945, I urged all those present to feel free to express themselves on any phase of the subject, scientific or political. Both General Marshall and I at this meeting expressed the view that atomic energy could not be considered simply in terms of military weapons but must also be considered in terms of a new relationship of man to the universe.

On June 1, after its discussions with the Scientific Panel, the Interim Committee unanimously adopted the following recommendations:

1. The bomb should be used against Japan as soon as possible.

2. It should be used on a dual target—that is, a military installation or war plant surrounded by or adjacent to houses and other buildings most susceptible to damage, and

3. It should be used without prior warning [of the nature of the weapon]. One member of the committee, Mr. [Ralph A.] Bard, later changed his view and dissented from recommendation.

In reaching these conclusions the Interim Committee carefully considered such alternatives as a detailed advance warning or a demonstration in some uninhabited area. Both of these suggestions were discarded as impractical. They were not regarded as likely to be effective in compelling a surrender of Japan, and both of them involved serious risks. Even the New Mexico test would not give final proof that any given bomb was certain to explode when dropped from an airplane. Quite apart from the generally unfamiliar nature of atomic explosives, there was the whole problem of exploding a bomb at a predetermined height in the air by a complicated mechanism which could not be tested in the static test of New Mexico. Nothing would have been more damaging to our effort to obtain surrender than a warning or a demonstration followed by a dud—and this was a real possibility. Furthermore, we had no bombs to waste. It was vital that a sufficient effect be quickly obtained with the few we had.

Need for a Tremendous Shock

The Interim Committee and the Scientific Panel also served as a channel through which suggestions from other scientists working on the atomic project were forwarded to me and to the President. Among the suggestions thus forwarded was one memorandum which questioned using the bomb at all against the enemy. On June 16, 1945, after consideration of that memorandum, the Scientific Panel made a report, from which I quote the following paragraphs:

> The opinions of our scientific colleagues on the initial use of these weapons are not unanimous: they range from the proposal of a purely technical demonstration to that of the military application best designed to induce surrender. Those who advocate a purely technical demonstration would wish to outlaw the use of atomic weapons, and have feared that if we use the weapons now our position in future negotiations will be prejudiced. Others emphasize the opportunity of saving American lives by immediate military use, and believe that such use

will improve the international prospects, in that they are more concerned with the prevention of war than with the elimination of this special weapon. We find ourselves closer to these latter views; *we can propose no technical demonstration likely to bring an end to the war; we see no acceptable alternative to direct military use.* [Italics mine]

With regard to these general aspects of the use of atomic energy, it is clear that we, as scientific men, have no proprietary rights. It is true that we are among the few citizens who have had occasion to give thoughtful consideration to these problems during the past few years. We have, however, no claim to special competence in solving the political, social, and military problems which are presented by the advent of atomic power.

The foregoing discussion presents the reasoning of the Interim Committee and its advisers. I have discussed the work of these gentlemen at length in order to make it clear that we sought the best advice that we could find. The committee's function was, of course, entirely advisory. The ultimate responsibility for the recommendation to the President rested upon me, and I have no desire to veil it. The conclusions of the committee were similar to my own, although I reached mine independently. I felt that to extract a genuine surrender from the Emperor and his military advisers, they must be administered a tremendous shock which would carry convincing proof of our power to destroy the Empire. Such an effective shock would save many times the number of lives, both American and Japanese, that it would cost. . . .

Advice to the President

I wrote a memorandum for the President, on July 2, which I believe fairly reprints the thinking of the American government as it finally took shape in action. This memorandum was prepared after discussion and general agreement with Joseph C. Grew, Acting Secretary of State, and Secretary of the Navy [James] Forrestal, and when I discussed it with the President, he expressed his general approval.

"Memorandum for the President, Proposed Program for Japan, July 2, 1945

"1. The plans of operation up to and including the first landing have been authorized and the preparations for the operation are now actually going on. This situation was accepted by all members of your conference on Monday, June 18.

"2. There is reason to believe that the operation for the occupation of Japan following the landing may be a very long, costly, and arduous struggle on our part. The terrain, much of which I have visited several times, has left the impression on my memory of being one which would be susceptible to a last ditch defense such as has been made on Iwo Jima and Okinawa and which of course is very much larger than either of those two areas. According to my recollection it will be much more unfavorable with regard to tank maneuvering than either the Philippines or Germany.

"3. If we once land on one of the main islands and begin a forceful occupation of Japan, we shall probably have cast the die of last ditch resistance. The Japanese are highly patriotic and certainly susceptible to calls for fanatical resistance to repel an invasion. Once started in actual invasion, we shall in my opinion have to go through with an even more bitter finish fight than in Germany. We shall incur the losses incident to such a war and we shall have to leave the Japanese islands even more thoroughly destroyed than was the case with Germany. This would be due both to the difference in the Japanese and German personal character and the differences in the size and character of the terrain through which the operations will take place.

"4. A question then comes: Is there any alternative to such a forceful occupation of Japan which will secure for us the equivalent of an unconditional surrender of her forces and a permanent destruction of her power again to strike an aggressive blow at the "peace of the Pacific"? I am inclined to think that there is enough such chance to make it well worthwhile our giving them a warning of what is to come and a definite opportunity to capitulate. As above suggested, it should be tried before the actual forceful occupation of the homeland islands is begun and furthermore the warning should be given in ample time to permit a national reaction to set in. . . .

"5. It is therefore my conclusion that a carefully timed warning be given to Japan by the chief representatives of the United States,

Great Britain, China, and, if then a belligerent, Russia by calling upon Japan to surrender and permit the occupation of her country in order to insure its complete demilitarization for the sake of the future peace.

"This warning should contain the following elements:

The varied and overwhelming character of the force we are about to bring to bear on the islands.

The inevitability and completeness of the destruction which the full application of this force will entail.

The determination of the Allies to destroy permanently all authority and influence of those who have deceived and misled the country into embarking on world conquest.

The determination of the Allies to limit Japanese sovereignty to her main islands and to render them powerless to mount and support another war.

The disavowal of any attempt to extirpate the Japanese as a race or to destroy them as a nation.

A statement of our readiness, once her economy is purged of its militaristic influence, to permit the Japanese to maintain such industries, particularly of a light consumer character, as offer no threat of aggression against their neighbors, but which can produce a sustaining economy, and provide a reasonable standard of living. The statement should indicate our willingness, for this purpose, to give Japan trade access to external raw materials, but no longer any control over the sources of supply outside her main islands. It should also indicate our willingness, in accordance with our now established foreign trade policy, in due course to enter into mutually advantageous trade relations with her.

The withdrawal from their country as soon as the above objectives of the Allies are accomplished, and as soon as there has been established a peacefully inclined government, of a character representative of the masses of the Japanese people. I personally think that if in saying this we should add that we do not exclude a constitutional monarchy under her present dynasty, it would substantially add to the chances of acceptance.

"6. Success of course will depend on the potency of the warning which we give her. She has an extremely sensitive national pride and, as we are now seeing every day, when actually locked with the enemy will fight to the very death. For that reason the warning must be tendered before the actual invasion has occurred and while the impending destruction, though clear beyond peradventure, has not yet reduced her to fanatical despair. If Russia is a part of the threat, the Russian attack, if actual, must not have progressed too far. Our own bombing should be confined to military objectives as far as possible."

It is important to emphasize the double character of the suggested warning. It was designed to promise destruction if Japan resisted, and hope, if she surrendered.

It will be noted that the atomic bomb is not mentioned in this memorandum. On grounds of secrecy the bomb was never mentioned except when absolutely necessary, and furthermore, it had not yet been tested. It was of course well forward in our minds, as the memorandum was written and discussed, that the bomb would be the best possible sanction if our warning were rejected.

The Bomb Was the Controlling Factor

The adoption of the policy outlined in the memorandum of July 2 was a decision of high politics; once it was accepted by the President, the position of the atomic bomb in our planning became quite clear. I find that I stated in my diary, as early as June 19, that "the last chance warning . . . must be given before an actual landing of the ground forces in Japan, and fortunately the plans provide for enough time to bring in the sanctions to our warning in the shape of heavy ordinary bombing attack and an attack of S-1." S-1 was a code name for the atomic bomb.

There was much discussion in Washington about the timing of the warning to Japan. The controlling factor in the end was the date already set for the Potsdam meeting of the Big Three. It was President Truman's decision that such a warning should be solemnly issued by the U.S. and the U.K. from this meeting, with the concurrence of the head of the Chinese government, so that it would be plain that *all* of Japan's principal enemies were in entire unity. This was done, in the Potsdam ultimatum of July 26, which very closely followed the above memorandum of July 2, with the exception that it made no mention of the Japanese Emperor.

On July 28 the Premier of Japan, [Kantaro] Suzuki, rejected the Potsdam ultimatum by announcing that it was "unworthy of public notice." In the face of this rejection we could only proceed to demonstrate that the ultimatum had meant exactly what it said when it stated that if the Japanese continued the war, "the full application of our military power, backed by our resolve, will mean the inevitable and complete destruction of the Japanese armed forces and just as inevitably the utter devastation of the Japanese homeland."

For such a purpose the atomic bomb was an eminently suitable weapon. The New Mexico test occurred while we were at Pots-

On August 6, 1945, the United States dropped an atomic bomb on Hiroshima, decimating the city and instantly killing some seventy thousand people.

dam, on July 16. It was immediately clear that the power of the bomb measured up to our highest estimates. We had developed a weapon of such a revolutionary character that its use against the enemy might well be expected to produce exactly the kind of shock on the Japanese ruling oligarchy which we desired, strengthening the position of those who wished peace, and weakening that of the military party. . . .

Hiroshima was bombed on August 6, and Nagasaki on August 9. These two cities were active working parts of the Japanese war effort. One was an army center; the other was naval and industrial. Hiroshima was the headquarters of the Japanese Army defending southern Japan and was a major military storage and assembly point. Nagasaki was a major seaport and it contained several large industrial plants of great wartime importance. We believed that our attacks had struck cities which must certainly be important to the Japanese military leaders, both Army and Navy, and we waited for a result. We waited one day.

Many accounts have been written about the Japanese surrender. After a prolonged Japanese cabinet session in which the deadlock was broken by the Emperor himself, the offer to surrender was made on August 10. It was based on the Potsdam terms, with a reservation concerning the sovereignty of the Emperor. While the Allied reply made no promises other than those already given, it implicitly recognized the Emperor's position by prescribing that his power must be subject to the orders of the Allied Supreme Commander. These terms were accepted on August 14 by the Japanese, and the instrument of surrender was formally signed on September 2 in Tokyo Bay. Our great objective was thus achieved, and all the evidence I have seen indicates that the controlling factor in the final Japanese decision to accept our terms of surrender was the atomic bomb. . . .

The Face of Death

In the foregoing pages I have tried to give an accurate account of my own personal observations of the circumstances which led up to the use of the atomic bomb and the reasons which underlay our use of it. To me they have always seemed compelling and clear, and I cannot see how any person vested with such responsibilities as mine could have taken any other course or given any other advice to his chiefs. . . .

As I read over what I have written, I am aware that much of it, in this year of peace, may have a harsh and unfeeling sound. It would perhaps be possible to say the same things and say them more gently. But I do not think it would be wise. As I look back over the five years of my service as Secretary of War, I see too many stern and heartrending decisions to be willing to pretend that war is anything else than what it is. The face of war is the face of death; death is an inevitable part of every order that a wartime leader gives. The decision to use the atomic bomb was a decision that brought death to over a hundred thousand Japanese. No explanation can change that fact and I do not wish to gloss it over. But this deliberate, premeditated destruction was our least abhorrent choice. The destruction of Hiroshima and Nagasaki put an end to the Japanese war. It stopped the fire raids and the strangling blockade; it ended the ghastly specter of a clash of great land armies.

In this last great action of the Second World War we were given final proof that war is death. War in the twentieth century has grown steadily more barbarous, more destructive, more debased in all its aspects. Now, with the release of atomic energy, man's ability to destroy himself is very nearly complete. The bombs dropped on Hiroshima and Nagasaki ended a war. They also made it wholly clear that we must never have another war. This is the lesson men and leaders everywhere must learn, and I believe that when they learn it they will find a way to lasting peace. There is no other choice.

Viewpoint 2

"With brutal disregard of any principle of humanity we 'demonstrated' the bomb on two great cities, utterly extinguishing them. This course has placed the United States in a bad light throughout the world."

Dropping the Atomic Bomb Was Unjustified

Christian Century

Following is part of an article that appeared in a Protestant journal, the *Christian Century*, only a few weeks after the United States dropped two atomic bombs on Japan, reducing the cities of Hiroshima and Nagasaki to rubble and killing more than one hundred thousand Japanese outright. The editors of the journal were most disturbed by the fact that the vast majority of those slain were civilians. The article first makes the point that Japan was already sufficiently defeated under a barrage of conventional weapons, so for the United States to resort to atomic weapons was unnecessary. The editors also present a moral argument against using the bomb, saying that it put the United States on the "moral defensive" in its future international dealings.

Christian Century, "America's Atomic Atrocity," August 29, 1945.

Something like a moral earthquake has followed the dropping of atomic bombs on two Japanese cities. Its continued tremors throughout the world have diverted attention even from the military victory itself. . . . It is our belief that the use made of the atomic bomb has placed our nation in an indefensible moral position.

We do not propose to debate the issue of military necessity, though the facts are clearly on one side of this issue. The atomic bomb was used at a time when Japan's navy was sunk, her airforce virtually destroyed, her homeland surrounded, her supplies cut off, and our forces poised for the final stroke. Recognition of her imminent defeat could be read between the lines of every Japanese communique. Neither do we intend to challenge Mr. Churchill's highly speculative assertion that the use of the bomb saved the lives of more than one million American and 250,000 British soldiers. We believe, however, that these lives could have been saved had our government followed a different course, more honorable and more humane. Our leaders seem not to have weighed the moral considerations involved. No sooner was the bomb ready than it was rushed to the front and dropped on two helpless cities, destroying more lives than the United States has lost in the entire war.

Perhaps it was inevitable that the bomb would ultimately be employed to bring Japan to the point of surrender. . . . But there was no military advantage in hurling the bomb upon Japan without warning. The least we might have done was to announce to our foe that we possessed the atomic bomb; that its destructive power was beyond anything known in warfare; and that its terrible effectiveness had been experimentally demonstrated in this country. We could thus have warned Japan of what was in store for her unless she surrendered immediately. If she doubted the good faith of our representations, it would have been a simple matter to select a demonstration target in the enemy's own country at a place where the loss of human life would be at a minimum.

If, despite such warning, Japan had still held out, we would have been in a far less questionable position had we then dropped the bombs on Hiroshima and Nagasaki. At least our record of deliberation and ample warning would have been clear. Instead, with brutal disregard of any principle of humanity we "demonstrated" the bomb on two great cities, utterly extinguishing them. This course has placed the United States in a bad light throughout the world. What the use of poison gas did to the reputation of Germany in World War I, the use of the atomic bomb has done for the reputation of the United States in World War II. Our future security is menaced by our own act, and our influence for justice and humanity in international affairs has been sadly crippled.

Japan's Moral Victory?

We have not heard the last of this in Japan itself. There a psychological situation is rapidly developing which will make the pacification of that land by our occupying forces—infinitely delicate and precarious at best—still more difficult and dubious. In these last days before the occupation by American forces, Japanese leaders are using their final hours of freedom of access to the radio to fix in the mind of their countrymen a psychological pattern which they hope will persist into an indefinite future. They reiterate that Japan has won a moral victory by not stooping as low as her enemies, that a lost war is regrettable but not necessarily irreparable, that the United States has been morally defeated because she has been driven to use unconscionable methods of fighting. They denounce the atomic bomb as the climax of barbarity and cite its use to prove how thin the veneer of Christian civilization is. They declare that Japan must bow to the conqueror at the emperor's command, but insist that she must devote all her available energies to scientific research. That of course can mean only one thing—research in methods of scientific destruction. Some officials have openly admonished the people to discipline themselves until the day of their revenge shall come.

Vengeance as a motive suffers from no moral or religious stigma in Japanese life. In the patriotic folklore of that land, no story is more popular than that of the Forty-Seven Ronin. It is a tale of revenge taken at the cost of their lives by the retainers of a feudal lord on an enemy who had treacherously killed their master. Every Japanese child knows that story. Until 1931, when Japan took Manchuria, the sacred obligation of retaliation was directed against the nations which had prevented Japanese expansion in that area and then had expanded their own holdings. After that it was aimed at white imperialism which was held to be the enemy of all people of color in the world, and particularly those in east Asia. In each case the justification of revenge was found in a real weakness in the moral position of the adversary. Our widespread use of the diabolic flame-thrower in combat, our scattering of millions of pounds of blazing jellied gasoline over wood and paper cities, and finally our employment of the atomic bomb give Japan the only justification she will require for once more seeking what she regards as justified revenge. . . .

America's Atomic Atrocity

The Japanese leaders are now in the act of creating a new myth as the carrier of the spirit of revenge. The myth will have much plausible ground in fact to support it. But its central core will be the story of the atomic bomb, hurled by the nation most reputed for its humanitarianism. Myths are hard to deal with. They lie embedded in the subconscious mind of a people, and reappear with vigor in periods of crisis. The story of the bomb will gather to itself the whole body of remembered and resented inconsistencies and false pretensions of the conquerors. The problem of spiritual rapprochement between the West and the Japanese will thus baffle the most wide and sensitive efforts of our occupying forces to find a solution. Yet our theory of occupation leaves us with no chance ever to let go of our vanquished foe until the roots of revenge have been extirpated. The outlook for the reconciliation of Germany with world civilization is ominous enough, but the outlook for the reconciliation of Japan is far more ominous. . . .

This act which has put the United States on the moral defensive has also put the Christian church on the defensive throughout the world and especially in Japan. . . .

The churches of America must dissociate themselves and their faith from this inhuman and reckless act of the American government. There is much that they can do, and it should be done speedily. They can give voice to the shame the American people feel concerning the barbaric methods used in their name in this war. In particular, in pulpits and conventions and other assemblies they can dissociate themselves from the government's use of the atomic bomb as an offensive weapon. They can demonstrate that the American people did not even know of the existence of such a weapon until it had been unleashed against an already beaten foe. By a groundswell of prompt protest expressing their outraged moral sense, the churches may enable the Japanese people, when the record is presented to them, to divorce the Christian community from any responsibility for America's atomic atrocity.

Viewpoint 3

"The stepped-up B-29 bombings [that would have occurred if the war continued] . . . would have cost the Japanese loss and suffering far, far greater than those inflicted by the two atomic bombs."

Dropping the Atomic Bomb Helped to End the War and Save Lives

Samuel Eliot Morison

For President Truman and other high American officials, one of the main arguments in favor of dropping a devastating new weapon—the atomic bomb—on Japan was the desire to save as many Allied and Japanese lives as possible. That argument is presented here by Samuel Eliot Morison, a Pulitzer Prize winner and one of the leading American historians of the twentieth century. He begins with a useful synopsis of the events leading up to the bombing of Hiroshima and Nagasaki, including diplomatic exchanges between the Japanese and Americans regarding the terms of Japan's surrender. Morison points out that many in

Samuel Eliot Morison, *Victory in the Pacific, 1945*. Boston: Little, Brown, and Company, 1960. Copyright © 1960 by Samuel Eliot Morison. Reproduced by permission of the publisher.

the Japanese high command wanted their countrymen to fight to the bitter end, which would have caused many deaths on both sides. He also includes Allied estimates of the death toll that might have been incurred had the atomic bomb not been used and an Allied invasion of Japan had ensued.

The Japanese people were never told that their country was losing the war; even our capture of such key points as Saipan, Manila, and Okinawa was explained as a strategic retirement. Hence, anyone high in the government or armed forces who recognized the symptoms of defeat found himself in a cruel dilemma. Love of country impelled him to seek a way out of the war, but admission of defeat exposed him to disgrace or assassination. Even the Emperor, who had always wished to preserve the peace, found himself caught in the same trap. When General [Douglas] Mac-Arthur after the war asked Hirohito [emperor of Japan] why he did not earlier take a stand against it, he made a symbolic gesture of his throat's being cut.

The Issue of Keeping the Emperor

Early in 1945, following the Allied invasion of Luzon [in the Philippines], the Emperor began to play an active part in the peace movement. His intervention had to be done cautiously and discreetly, so as not to disturb the established tradition and machinery of government. In late January and early February he conferred individually with seven of the *jushin*, the "important subjects"—former Premiers and presidents of the Privy Council. He found their feeling to be like his, that an early peace was necessary. Prince Konoye, the former Premier, stated bluntly that Japan faced certain defeat and urged his cousin the Emperor to take positive action to end the war.

Fear of the powerful military clique was so pervasive that nothing could be done until early April, when the invasion of Okinawa, and Russia's denunciation of the Soviet-Japanese neutrality pact, precipitated a new crisis. When General [Kuniaki] Koiso resigned the premiership on 5 April 1945, the *jushin* provided his relief.

These men now had the confidence of the Lord Keeper, Marquis Kido, closest adviser and personal friend of the Emperor, who gave his approval to a political deal. The new Premier, who took office on 7 April, was the octogenarian Baron Kantaro Suzuki. . . . It was ironic that, on the very day he took office, the battleship *Yamato* was sunk. Shigenori Togo, also an advocate of peace, was appointed Foreign Minister.

The Army chiefs insisted, as their price for allowing Suzuki to form a cabinet, that he prosecute the war to a victorious finish. Consequently, the new Premier had to pretend to be doing just that. He knew that he was expected by the Emperor to bring the war to an end; but, as he held office at the Army's sufferance, he had to continue making die-hard public pronouncements.

Although it takes but one antagonist to start a war, at least two are required to conclude peace; so it is natural to inquire what, if anything, the United States and the other Allies were doing about it. The answer is, almost nothing, except to press the war more and more vigorously. It is possible that if President Roosevelt had lived six weeks longer, he would have taken the advice of Joseph C. Grew [the former U.S. ambassador to Japan] to give public assurance that if Japan surrendered "unconditionally," she could keep her Emperor. The Department of State had envisaged just that, even at the beginning of the war. Following this line, government agencies in propaganda for home consumption had consistently ignored Hirohito and directed popular rage and hatred against [War Minister Hideki] Tojo and his military clique. This attitude was due in part to knowledge by the insiders that Hirohito had never wanted war; partly to experience of World War I, in which the Kaiser was played up as principal culprit, and his removal led to a weak government which was overthrown by Hitler. The Imperial Palace had been conspicuously spared in the successive bombings of Tokyo; and owing to the Secretary of War's insistence, the Army Air Force had not bombed the two principal religious and artistic centers in Japan, Nikko and Kyoto.

Mr. Grew . . . detected through the double talk of the Suzuki government a genuine desire to end the war. He knew that the one essential gesture to help the peace party in Japan was to promise as a condition of peace that the Emperor would not be deposed.

From 20 December 1944, Mr. Grew was undersecretary of state. He found that many top people in the department did not share his views. A popular demand, "Hirohito must go," was being whipped up by a section of the American press and by certain columnists and radio commentators. Admiral Leahy observed that some of the civilians who had access to the President wanted Hirohito to be tried as a war criminal, and the nationalist press in China demanded that he be hanged. The Soviet government, of course, aimed to break up the imperial system, so that Communism could profit from the ensuing anarchy.

After hearing reports of the destructive bombing raids on Tokyo of 23 and 25 May 1945, Mr. Grew called on the President and begged him to make an explicit statement, in an address that he was planning to deliver on the thirty-first, that Hirohito could retain his throne if Japan surrendered. Harry Truman, who had been in the presidential office only six weeks, was sympathetic but felt unqualified to make so vital a policy pronouncement without military advice. At his request Mr. Grew consulted General Marshall and Secretaries [James V.] Forrestal and [Henry L.] Stimson. They, too, were sympathetic, but advised against making any such assurance at that time, because the Okinawa campaign had almost bogged down and the Japanese government would interpret any such statement as evidence of war weariness on our part. So this opportunity to proffer a friendly hand to Japanese advocates of peace was missed. It is very unlikely that it would have been accepted, since the Japanese military and naval chiefs were against concluding peace even after two atomic bombs had been dropped and explicit assurances about the Emperor had been given. . . .

Unconditional Surrender?

Then, out of a clear sky, on a summer day of sweltering heat, came the Potsdam Declaration of 26 July by President Truman, Prime Minister Churchill, and Chiang Kai-shek, stating the conditions under which Japan would be called upon to surrender "unconditionally." The principal terms of the Potsdam Declaration were:

1. The authority and influence of the Japanese militarists "must be eliminated for all time."

2. Until a "new order of peace, security and justice" is established in Japan, Allied forces will occupy Japanese key points "to secure the achievement" of this basic objective. . . .

3. Japanese sovereignty will be limited to Hokkaido, Honshu, Kyushu, Shikoku, and adjacent smaller islands.

4. Japanese military forces, "after being completely disarmed, shall be permitted to return to their homes with the opportunity to lead peaceful and productive lives."

5. "We do not intend that the Japanese shall be enslaved as a race or destroyed as a nation, but stern justice shall be meted out to all war criminals. . . . Freedom of speech, of religion, and of thought, as well as respect for the fundamental human rights, shall be established."

6. Japan may retain such industries as will sustain her economy, but may not rearm; and she may look forward to "participation in world trade relations."

7. Occupation forces "shall be withdrawn from Japan as soon as these objectives have been accomplished and there has been established a peacefully inclined and responsible government."

8. The Japanese government is called upon "to proclaim now the unconditional surrender of all Japanese armed forces." The alternative is "prompt and utter destruction."

A broadcast of this declaration, received in Tokyo on 27 July, caused a flurry of discussion in high governmental circles as to how it should be handled. Foreign Minister Togo wished to play a waiting game and avoid any official statement. For (a typically Japanese condition), if any official declaration were made, it would have to be a flat rejection, to please the military men in the cabinet. Unfortunately, Premier Suzuki upset the applecart when, at a press conference on 28 July, he indicated that the cabinet considered the Potsdam Declaration to be a mere rehash of the earlier and unacceptable Cairo Declaration, and as such unworthy of official notice. And, he added, the increase of aircraft production gave renewed hope of a Japanese victory.

No explicit assurance about the Emperor had issued from Potsdam; but (so Shigemitsu, Foreign Minister in the Koiso government, assured me in 1950) the reference in paragraph seven to withdrawing occupation forces after a "peacefully inclined and responsible government" had been set up indicated to the Japanese that they would be permitted to determine their own future.

"The Greatest Thing in History"

If the Suzuki government could have made up its mind promptly to accept the Potsdam Declaration as a basis for peace, there would have been no explosion of an atomic bomb over Japan. . . .

The President had already decided to use the bomb if Japan did not accept the declaration and on 24 July had issued the necessary order to the Army Air Force to "deliver its first special bomb as soon as weather will permit visual bombing after about 3 August.". . .

The B-29 nicknamed "Enola Gay," commanded by Colonel Paul W. Tibets, U.S.A., was chosen to carry the first atomic bomb. Captain William S. Parsons, a Navy ordnance specialist who had had charge of the ordnance aspects of the bomb and of its safety features, came along to assemble it and make the final adjustments en route.

At 0245 August 6 "Enola Gay" took off from North Field, Tinian, followed by two observation planes. Over Iwo Jima it began a slow climb to 30,000 feet. At 0730 Captain Parsons and his assistant made final adjustments on the bomb. Weather reconnaissance planes reported all clear over Hiroshima. The B-29 was over the city at 0911, when controls were passed to the bombardier, Major Thomas W. Ferebee, U.S.A., who at 0915 "toggled the bomb out" at an altitude of 31,600 feet and speed of 328 m.p.h. No enemy planes attacked "Enola Gay." She landed on Tinian at 1458.

Results were catastrophic. The bomb exploded right over a parade ground where the Japanese Second Army was doing calisthenics. The soldiers were wiped out almost to a man. Everything in the city within an area of over four square miles was razed or fused. An estimated 71,379 people, including the military, were killed; 19,691 were seriously injured; and about 171,000 rendered homeless. This seems, however, to have been an overestimate. A Japanese official notice of 31 July 1959 stated that the total number of deaths attributed to the bombing of Hiroshima, including all that had occurred in the nearly 14 years since it happened, was 60,175.

President Truman got the word at noon on 6 August (west longitude date) on board cruiser *Augusta* while crossing the Atlantic.

He told the officers and men about it, saying, "This is the greatest thing in history."

The Japanese Make an Offer

Before sunrise 9 August the Russian declaration of war on Japan was known in Tokyo. At 1000 Marquis Kido conveyed to Premier Suzuki the Emperor's belief that it was urgent to accept the Potsdam Declaration immediately. The S.C.D.W. [Japan's supreme war council] promptly summoned to the Imperial Palace, was already in session when the second atomic bomb exploded over Nagasaki, at 1101. All agreed to insist that the prerogatives of the imperial family be preserved, but beyond that there was no agreement. War Minister General Anami, Army Chief of Staff General Umezu, and Admiral Toyoda, the Navy Chief of Staff, insisted on three conditions: 1) the Japanese would disarm their own troops overseas, 2) war criminals would be prosecuted by Japanese courts, and 3) only a limited military occupation of Japan would be permitted. Togo pointed out that the Allies were certain to refuse such conditions, that all hope of Japanese victory had vanished, and that Japan must no longer delay seeking peace. But as Anami, Umezu, and Toyoda held out, nothing could be decided. . . .

Since an Imperial Conference had no formal power to decide anything, a cabinet meeting was called at about 0300 August 10. There, the imperial decision was unanimously approved.

At 0700 August 10, a message was sent to the governments of the United States, Great Britain, the Soviet Union, and China, stating that Japan was ready to accept the terms of the Potsdam Declaration with the understanding that the prerogatives of the Emperor as a sovereign ruler were not prejudiced. . . .

[In reply, the Americans demanded the following conditions:]

1. "From the moment of surrender the authority of the Emperor and Japanese government . . . shall be subject to the Supreme Commander of the Allied Powers who will take such steps as he deems proper to effectuate the surrender terms."

2. The Emperor will authorize his government and Imperial General Headquarters to sign the surrender and shall command all his armed forces to lay down their arms.

3. Immediately upon the surrender the Japanese government

shall transport prisoners of war and interned civilians to places of safety where they can be embarked in Allied transports.

4. The ultimate form of the government of Japan shall be established by the free will of the Japanese people.

5. Allied occupation forces will remain in Japan "until the purposes set forth in the Potsdam Declaration are achieved.". . .

The Surrender

During the night of 13 to 14 August, seven B-29s dropped on Tokyo more than five million leaflets, containing the text of the Japanese note accepting the Potsdam Declaration and a Japanese translation of [the American] reply. This was the first intimation the people had of what was going on. At 0830 August 14, Marquis Kido brought one of these leaflets to the Emperor and urgently advised him to take prompt action, predicting that the leaflets would have a profound effect. Unless the Emperor declared immediately for peace, he might lose control of armed forces in the field. . . .

In a highly emotional atmosphere, Anami, Umezu, and Toyoda repeated their earlier arguments for continuing to fight. The Emperor then spoke the thoughts that he had long firmly held. Continuing the war, he said, will merely result in additional destruction. The whole nation will be reduced to ashes. The Allied reply is a virtually complete acknowledgment of the position of his note of 0700 August 10 and evidence "of the peaceful and friendly intentions of the enemy." It is the imperial desire that his ministers of state accept it. They will at once prepare an imperial rescript broadcasting this decision directly to the people.

The deed was done. At 1449 August 14 Radio Tokyo flashed the Emperor's decision around the world. The cabinet was already making a final draft of the rescript, which had been in preparation since 10 August. At 2100 it was completed and taken to the Emperor, who signed it at 2250 August 14. Ten minutes later it was officially proclaimed that Japan would accept the Allied terms, and a note to that effect was sent to the Allied governments through a neutral country. This important news reached President Truman at 1550 August 14, west longitude date. He announced it from the White House at 1900 the same day and declared a two-day holiday of jubilation. . . .

Determined to Die Fighting

It was the Emperor who cut governmental red tape and made the great decision. This required courage. The Army chiefs and Admiral Toyoda were not greatly moved by the atomic explosions. They argued that the two bombs were probably all that the United States had, and if more were made, we would not dare use them when invading Japan; that there was a fair chance of defeating the invasion by massed kamikaze attacks; and that, in any event, national honor demanded a last battle on Japanese soil. All the fighting hitherto had been little more than peripheral skirmishes; the way to victory was to "lure" the Americans ashore and "annihilate" them. . . .

On the Allied side, it has been argued that the maritime blockade, virtually complete by mid-August, would have strangled Japanese economy and that the B-29s and naval gunfire ships would have destroyed its principal cities and forced a surrender before long, without the aid of the atomic bombs or of invasion. Fleet Admirals King and Leahy lent their distinguished advocacy to this view. Whether or not they were correct, not even time can tell. But of some things, one can be sure. The stepped-up B-29 bombings and naval bombardments, had they been continued after 15 August, would have cost the Japanese loss and suffering far, far greater than those inflicted by the two atomic bombs. And the probable effects of the projected invasions of Kyushu and Honshu in the fall and winter of 1945 to 1946 and of a desperate place-to-place defense of Japan stagger the imagination. It is simply not true that Japan had no military capability left in mid-August. Although 2550 kamikaze planes had been expended, there were 5350 of them still left, together with as many more ready for orthodox use and some 7000 under repair or in storage; and 5000 young men were training for the Kamikaze Corps. The plan was to disperse all aircraft on small grass strips in Kyushu, Shikoku, and western Honshu and in underground hangars and caves and to conserve them for kamikaze crashes on the Allied amphibious forces invading the home islands. Considering the number of planes, pilots, and potential targets, all within a short distance of principal airfields, it requires little imagination to depict the horrible losses that would have been inflicted on the invading forces, even before they got ashore. After the landing, there would have been protracted battles on Japanese soil which would have cost each side very many more lives and created a bitterness which even time could hardly have healed. Japan had plenty of ammunition left; the U.S. Army after the war found thousands of tons holed up in Hokkaido alone. And, as Russia would have been a full partner in this final campaign, there is a fair chance that Japan would have been divided like Germany and Korea, if not delivered completely to the mercy of the Communists.

We must also point out that, even after two atomic bombs had been dropped, the Potsdam Declaration clarified, the guards' insurrection defeated, and the Emperor's will made known, it was touch and go whether the Japanese actually would surrender. Hirohito had to send members of the imperial family to the principal Army commands to ensure compliance. His younger brother, Prince Takamatsu, was just in time to make the Atsugi airfield available for the first occupation forces on 26 August and to keep the kamikaze boys grounded. They were boasting that they would crash the *Missouri* when she entered Tokyo Bay. If these elements had had their way, the war would have been resumed, with the Allies feeling that the Japanese were hopelessly treacherous and with a savagery on both sides that is painful to contemplate.

When these facts and events of the Japanese surrender are known and weighed, it will become evident that the atomic bomb was the keystone of a very fragile arch.

Viewpoint 4

"In the eyes of the world the atomic bomb has cost us dearly. . . . We no longer are the world's moral leader."

The Atomic Bombing of Japan Was Unnecessary and Avoidable

Hanson W. Baldwin

Some modern scholars and other observers are not convinced that the use of the atomic bomb on Japan during World War II was justified. Many in this camp agree with the writings of Hanson W. Baldwin, a noted editor covering military affairs for the *New York Times* during the years following World War II. In his view, presented in the following essay, Japan was already beaten, or nearly so, before the atomic bombs devastated the cities of Hiroshima and Nagasaki. Baldwin suggests that these frightening weapons were used less for military necessity than to provide the United States more leverage in peace negotiations and postwar relations. He also expresses the view that using the atomic bomb cost the United States "the preeminent moral position we once occupied."

Hanson W. Baldwin, *Great Mistakes of the War*. New York: Collins, Knowlton-Wing, 1950. Copyright © 1950 by Hanson W. Baldwin. Reproduced by permission.

The utilization of the atomic bomb against a prostrate and defeated Japan in the closing days of the war exemplifies . . . the narrow, astigmatic concentration of our planners upon one goal, and one alone: victory.

Nowhere in all of [the] forceful and eloquent apologia for the leveling of Hiroshima and Nagasaki is there any evidence of an ulterior. . . .

To accept the . . . thesis that the atomic bomb should have been used as it was used, it is necessary first to accept the contention that the atomic bomb achieved or hastened victory, and second, and more important, that it helped to consolidate the peace or to further the political aims for which war was fought.

History can accept neither contention.

The Bomb Used in Haste?

Let us examine the first. The atomic bomb was dropped in August. Long before that month started our forces were securely based in Okinawa, the Marianas and Iwo Jima; Germany had been defeated; our fleet had been cruising off the Japanese coast with impunity bombarding the shoreline; our submarines were operating in the Sea of Japan; even inter-island ferries had been attacked and sunk. Bombing, which started slowly in June, 1944, from China bases and from the Marianas in November, 1944, had been increased materially in 1945, and by August, 1945, more than 16,000 tons of bombs had ravaged Japanese cities. Food was short; mines and submarines and surface vessels and planes clamped an iron blockade around the main islands; raw materials were scarce. Blockade, bombing, and unsuccessful attempts at dispersion had reduced Japanese production capacity from 20 to 60 per cent. The enemy, in a military sense, was in a hopeless strategic position by the time the Potsdam demand for unconditional surrender was made on July 26.

Such, then, was the situation when we wiped out Hiroshima and Nagasaki.

Need we have done it? No one can, of course, be positive, but the answer is almost certainly negative.

The invasion of Japan, which Admiral Leahy had opposed as too wasteful of American blood, and in any case unnecessary, was scheduled (for the southern island of Kyushu) for Nov. 1, 1945, to be followed if necessary, in the spring of 1946, by a major landing on the main island of Honshu. We dropped the two atomic bombs in early August, almost two months before our first D-Day. The decision to drop them. . . . followed the recommendations of [American] Secretary [of War Henry] Stimson and an "Interim Committee" of distinguished officials and scientists, who had found "no acceptable alternative to direct military use."

But the weakness of this statement is inherent, for none was tried and "military use" of the bomb was undertaken despite strong opposition to this course by numerous scientists and Japanese experts, including former Ambassador Joseph Grew. Not only was the Potsdam ultimatum merely a restatement of the politically impossible—unconditional surrender—but it could hardly be construed as a direct warning of the atomic bomb and was not taken as such by anyone who did not know the bomb had been created. A technical demonstration of the bomb's power may well have been unfeasible, but certainly a far more definite warning could have been given; and it is hard to believe that a target objective in Japan with but sparse population could not have been found. The truth is we did not try; we gave no specific warning. There were almost two months before our scheduled invasion of Kyushu, in which American ingenuity could have found ways to bring home to the Japanese the impossibility of their position and the horrors of the weapon being held over them; yet we rushed to use the bomb as soon as unconditional surrender was rejected. Had we devised some demonstration or given a more specific warning than the Potsdam ultimatum, and had the Japanese still persisted in continued resistance after some weeks of our psychological offensive, we should perhaps have been justified in the bomb's use; at least, our hands would have been more clean.

Twice Guilty

But, in fact, our only warning to a Japan already militarily defeated, and in a hopeless situation, was the Potsdam demand for unconditional surrender issued on July 26, when we knew Japanese surrender attempts had started. Yet when the Japanese surrender was negotiated about two weeks later, after the bomb was dropped, our unconditional surrender demand was made conditional and we agreed, as Stimson had originally proposed we should do, to continuation of the Emperor upon his imperial throne.

We were, therefore, twice guilty. We dropped the bomb at a time when Japan already was negotiating for an end of the war but before those negotiations could come to fruition. We demanded unconditional surrender, then dropped the bomb and accepted conditional surrender, a sequence which indicates pretty clearly that the Japanese would have surrendered, even if the bomb had not been dropped, had the Potsdam Declaration included our promise to permit the Emperor to remain on his imperial throne.

What we now know of the condition of Japan, and of the days preceding her final surrender on Aug. 15, verifies these conclusions. It is clear, in retrospect, (and was understood by some, notably Admiral Leahy, at the time) that Japan was militarily on her last legs. Yet our intelligence estimates greatly overstated her strength.

The background for surrender had been sketched in fully, well before the bombs were dropped, and the Strategic Bombing Survey declares that "interrogation of the highest Japanese officials, following V-J Day, indicated that Japan would have surrendered . . . even . . . if the atomic bombs had not been dropped." "Even before the large-scale bombing of Japan was initiated, the raw material base of Japanese industry was effectively undermined. An accelerated decline of armament production was inevitable."

Admiral Chester W. Nimitz, in a talk to the National Geographic Society on January 25, 1946, declared, "I am convinced that the complete impunity with which the Pacific Fleet pounded Japan at pointblank range was the decisive factor in forcing the Japanese to ask the Russians to approach us for peace proposals in July.

"Meanwhile, aircraft from our new fields in the Okinawa group were daily shuttling back and forth over Kyushu and Shokoku and B-29's of the Twentieth Air Force were fire-bombing major Japanese cities. . . .

"The atomic bomb merely hastened a process already reaching an inevitable conclusion. . . ."

There can be no doubt that this conclusion of Admiral Nimitz will be the verdict of history. Militarily, we "killed" Japan in many different ways: by crushing defeats at sea and on land; by the strangulation of the blockade of which the principal instrument was the submarine; by bombing with conventional bombs. After the seizure of Okinawa—probably even before that—the blockade alone could have defeated Japan; was, indeed, defeating her. Admiral Leahy was right; invasion was not necessary. . . .

In the words of a well known Japanese correspondent, Masuo Kato, who was in Washington for the Domei News Agency when the war started: "The thunderous arrival of the first atomic bomb at Hiroshima was only a *coup de gráce* for an empire already struggling in particularly agonizing death throes. The world's newest and most devastating of weapons had floated out of the summer sky to destroy a city at a stroke, but its arrival had small effect on the outcome of the war between Japan and the United Nations."

It is therefore clear today—and was clear to many even as early as the spring of 1945—that the military defeat of Japan was certain; the atomic bomb was not needed.

Did the Bomb Shorten the War?

But if the bomb did not procure victory, did it hasten it?

This question cannot be answered with equal precision, particularly since the full story of the Japanese surrender attempts has not been compiled. But a brief chronology of known events indicates that the atomic bomb may have shortened the war by a few days—not more.

The day before Christmas, 1944 (two months *before* the Yalta conference), U.S. intelligence authorities in Washington received a report from a confidential agent in Japan that a peace party was emerging and that the Koiso cabinet would soon be succeeded by a cabinet headed by Admiral Baron Suzuki who would initiate surrender proceedings.

The Koiso cabinet *was* succeeded by a new government headed by Suzuki in early April, 1945, but even prior to this significant change, the Japanese—in February, 1945—had approached the Russians with a request that they act as intermediary in arranging a peace with the Western powers. The Russian Ambassador, Malik, in Tokyo, was the channel of the approach. The Russians, however, set their price of mediation so high that the Japanese

temporarily dropped the matter. The United States was not officially informed of this approach until after the end of the war.

Prior to, coincident with, and after this February attempt, ill-
defined peace approaches were made through the Japanese Ambassadors in Stockholm and Moscow, particularly Moscow. These
approaches were so informal, and to some extent represented to
such a degree the personal initiative of the two Ambassadors concerned, that they never came to a head.

But after a meeting with Stalin in Moscow on May 27, before
the trial A-bomb was even tested in New Mexico, Harry Hopkins
cabled President Truman that:

1. "Japan is doomed and the Japanese know it.

2. "Peace feelers are being put out by certain elements in
Japan. . . ."

The first atomic bomb was dropped on Hiroshima on August
6; Russia entered the war on August 8; and the second atomic
bomb was dropped on Nagasaki on August 9. . . .

But neither the people of Japan nor their leaders were as impressed with the atomic bomb as were we. The public did not
know until after the war what had happened to Hiroshima; and
even so, they had endured fire raids against Tokyo which had
caused more casualties than the atomic bomb and had devastated
a greater area than that destroyed at Hiroshima. The Supreme
War Direction Council was initially told that a fragment of the Hiroshima bomb indicated that it was made in Germany (!), that it
appeared to be a conventional explosive of great power, and that
there was only one bomb available. . . .

In other words, the bomb changed no opinions; the Emperor
himself, who had already favored peace, broke the deadlock.

"If nobody else has any opinion to express," Hirohito said, "we
would express our own. We demand that you will agree to it. We
see only one way left for Japan to save herself. That is the reason
we have made this determination to endure the unendurable and
suffer the insufferable."

A Whirlwind of Hate

. . . It is quite possible that the atomic bombs shortened the war
by a day, a week, or a month or two—not more.

But at what a price! For whether or not the atomic bomb hastened victory, it is quite clear it has not won the peace.

Some may point to the comparative tranquility of Japan under MacArthur in the postwar period as due in part to the terror of American arms created by the bomb. This is scarcely so; Japan's seeming tranquility is a surface one which has been furthered by a single occupation authority and the nature of the Japanese people. But I venture to estimate that those who suffered at Hiroshima and Nagasaki will never forget it, and that we sowed there a whirlwind of hate which we shall someday reap.

In estimating the effect of the use of the bomb upon the peace, we must remember, first, that we used the bomb for one purpose, and one only: not to secure a more equable peace, but to hasten victory. By using the bomb we have become identified, rightfully or wrongly, as inheritors of the mantle of Genghis Khan and all those of past history who have justified the use of utter ruthlessness in war.

It may well be argued, of course, that war—least of all modern war—knows no humanity, no rules, and no limitations, and that death by the atomic bomb is no worse than death by fire bombs or high explosives or gas or flame throwers. It is, of course, true that the atomic bomb is no worse qualitatively than other lethal weapons; it is merely quantitatively more powerful; other weapons cause death in fearful ways; the atomic bomb caused more deaths. We already had utilized fire raids, mass bombardment of cities, and flame throwers in the name of expediency and victory prior to August 6, even though many of our people had recoiled from such practices.

Even as late as June 1, 1945, Stimson "had sternly questioned his Air Forces leader, wanting to know whether the apparently indiscriminate bombings of Tokyo were absolutely necessary. Perhaps, as he [Stimson] later said, he was misled by the constant talk of 'precision bombing,' but he had believed that even air power could be limited in its use by the old concept of 'legitimate military targets.' Now in the conflagration bombings by massed B-29's, he was permitting a kind of total war he had always hated, and in recommending the use of the atomic bomb he was implicitly confessing that there could be no significant limits to the horror of modern war."

If we accept this confession—that there can be no limits set to modern war—we must also accept the bitter inheritance of Genghis Khan and the mantles of all the other ruthless despoilers of the past.

We Have Lost Morally

In reality, we took up where these great conquerors left off long before we dropped the atomic bomb. Americans, in their own eyes, are a naively idealistic people, with none of the crass ruthlessness so often exhibited by other nations. Yet in the eyes of others our record is very far from clean, nor can objective history palliate it. Rarely have we been found on the side of restricting horror; too often we have failed to support the feeble hands of those who would limit war. We did not ratify the Hague convention of 1899, outlawing the use of dumdum (expanding) bullets in war. . . . At the time the war in the Pacific ended, pressure for the use of gas against Japanese island positions had reached the open discussion stage, and rationalization was leading surely to justification, an expedient justification since we had air superiority and the means to deluge the enemy with gas, while he had no similar way to reply. We condemned the Japanese for their alleged use of biological agents against the Chinese, yet in July and August, 1945, a shipload of U.S. biological agents for use in destruction of the Japanese rice crop was en route to the Marianas. . . .

Yet surely these methods—particularly the extension of unrestricted warfare to enemy civilians—defeated any peace aims we might have had, and had little appreciable effect in hastening military victory. For in any totalitarian state, the leaders rather than the peoples must be convinced of defeat, and the indiscriminate use of mass or area weapons, like biological agents and the atomic bomb, strike at the people, not the rulers. We cannot succeed, therefore, by such methods, in drawing that fine line between ruler and ruled that ought to be drawn in every war; we cannot hasten military victory by slaughtering the led; such methods only serve to bind the led closer to their leaders. Moreover, unrestricted warfare can never lay the groundwork for a more stable peace. Its heritage may be the salt-sown fields of Carthage, or the rubble and ruin of a Berlin or Tokyo or Hiroshima; but neither economically nor psychologically can unrestricted warfare—atomic warfare or biological warfare—lead anywhere save to eventual disaster.

During the . . . conflict we brought new horror to the meaning of war; the ruins of Germany and Japan, the flame-scarred tissues of the war-wounded attest our efficiency. And on August 6, 1945, that blinding flash above Hiroshima wrote a climax to an era of American expediency. On that date we joined the list of those who had introduced new and horrible weapons for the extermination of man; we joined the Germans who had first utilized gas, the Japanese with their biological agents, the Huns and the Mongols who had made destruction a fine art.

It is my contention that in the eyes of the world the atomic bomb has cost us dearly; we have lost morally; we no longer are the world's moral leader as in the days of the Wilsonian Fourteen Points. It is my contention that the unlimited destruction caused by our unlimited methods of waging war has caused us heavy economic losses in the forms of American tax subsidies to Germany and Japan. It is my contention that unrestricted warfare and unlimited aims cost us politically the winning of the peace. . . .

The use of the atomic bomb, therefore, cost us dearly; we are now branded with the mark of the beast. Its use may have hastened victory—though by very little—but it has cost us in peace the pre-eminent moral position we once occupied. Japan's economic troubles are in some degree the result of unnecessary devastation. We have embarked upon Total War with a vengeance; we have done our best to make it far more total. If we do not soon reverse this trend, if we do not cast about for means to limit and control war, if we do not abandon the doctrine of expediency, of unconditional surrender, of total victory, we shall someday ourselves become the victims of our own theories and practices.

CHAPTER 4

Did the Allies Fight World War II Morally and Effectively?

✸ Chapter Preface

World War II was a global struggle that affected the lives of hundreds of millions of people in various and often very different ways. So it is not surprising that retrospective views of the war vary considerably. A majority of people today probably believe that the conflict was fought largely to defeat some dangerous totalitarian regimes and thereby to safeguard human freedom around the world. However, some people feel that in the long run the war did not make the world either safer or more free. On the one hand, they say, the tremendous arms race spurred on by the conflict continued after its conclusion. This military buildup resulted in a decades-long nuclear standoff between the United States and the Soviet Union that could have erupted into a global catastrophe at any given moment. Also, say critics of the war, the Soviet Union, hardly a bastion of freedom, received a huge boost from the Allied victory. As Robert Higgs of the Independent Institute puts it:

> World War II did not end in a victory for the forces of freedom; to an equal or greater extent, the defeat of Nazi Germany and its allies represented a victory for the forces of totalitarian oppression in the Soviet Union and, later, its surrogates around the world. Hence, in 1945 we merely traded one set of aggressive enemies for another.

However one views the effectiveness of the war in terms of safeguarding humanity or freedom, one cannot argue about the economic significance of the conflict for later generations. First, the war cost billions to prosecute and billions more went into the massive recovery and rebuilding efforts that followed it. More importantly, at war's end the geopolitical map of the world had been radically redrawn. For the first time in centuries, the main focus of world power had shifted away from Europe. Though the European sphere remained important in world affairs, the United States emerged as the globe's first true superpower, not only militarily but also economically. The Soviet Union soon rivaled the United States in military terms; but the Soviets, with their largely state-controlled economy, were never able to match the economic output of the United States, with its enormous, adaptable, and resilient market economy. For this and other reasons, the Soviet Union eventually collapsed, leaving the United States as the world's lone superpower.

Meanwhile, throughout most of the postwar era the American economy grew larger and stronger, which led to a sharp rise in living standards in the United States, especially among the members of the swiftly expanding middle class. Tens of millions of people were able to own their own homes, buy two cars, and send their children to college, a level and scale of prosperity previously unheard-of in any nation.

At the same time, the American economy became increasingly intertwined with and dependent on foreign markets and workers. This interdependence had the inevitable effect of influencing the manner in which other nations did business. It also made America's affluent society a sort of model to be envied and copied. In the words of widely read political scholars James Hoge and Fareed Zakaria, in many parts of the world everyday life has come to be

> dominated by the idea and the reality of America's distinctive creed, liberal democratic capitalism. Nations and peoples of every culture are adapting their old world to these new ideas, and their countries are being revolutionized, slowly but surely, by it. Some of this transformation is the result of broad structural shifts like industrialization and modernization, but much of it is the result of one nation's efforts to stand for and fight for certain political and economic ideals. The American encounter has changed the world.

The "American encounter," as these writers call it, did not begin with World War II. But that conflict gave the United States the enormous political and economic boost it needed to transform its latent potential as a superpower into reality. For better or worse, to the joy of some and the bitterness of others, America's incredible success story and economic dominance is a reality of the modern world that cannot be ignored. That reality transcends all other arguments about the effectiveness and legacy of the Second World War even as it leads the peoples of the world toward an uncertain future.

Viewpoint 1

"Americans were not cruel, or evil, or monstrous in the sense that Hitler was. They simply did not care [about the plight of European Jews]."

The United States and the Allies Could Have Done More to Avert the Holocaust

Katherine E. Culbertson

In this article written for a well-known historical journal, researcher Katherine E. Culbertson charges that neither the United States nor any of the other major Allied nations who fought World War II did enough to address the plight of European Jews, who all through the war were being exterminated by Adolf Hitler's murderous Nazi regime. Citing David Wyman, Paul Johnson, Robert Dallek, and other noted historians, Culbertson suggests that American and other Allied officials did know that the Holocaust was under way, but decided that their best course of action was to put all their resources into defeating Germany. She is particularly harsh in her criticism of President Roosevelt, endorsing Wyman's charge that his failure to do more to save Europe's Jews was the "worst failure" of his presidency.

Katherine E. Culbertson, "American Wartime Indifference to the Plight of the European Jews," *Hanover Historical Review*, vol. 2, Spring 1994. Copyright © 1994 by the *Hanover Historical Review*. Reproduced by permission.

From 1942 until 1945, America and the rest of the Allied world failed to heed [the] call for help [from European Jews marked for persecution and death by the Nazis]. Armed with complete knowledge of the massacre and resources to alleviate the tragedy, America lacked only the will to spare the lives of millions of Jews and other undesired inhabitants of Hitler's Europe. To account for its inattention to the problem, the United States unleashed a flurry of excuses. Over the course of the war, the most popular rationalization became the supremacy of war aims over the incidental needs of non-enemy civilians. The frequency and intensity with which American officials invoked this reason reflected the larger mentality implicit in American involvement in World War II. The hardening of warriors to the cries of downtrodden Jews in Europe represented America's flight from moral responsibility and a retreat from its own standards of humanitarianism. Examining wartime behavior and attitudes in the United States regarding the hapless Jews of Europe dismantles one of the most imbedded myths in post-war America, that the United States, as a boundless well of democracy and freedom always outstretching its arms to those seeking refuge, entered the war to in part fulfill that pledge. As Emma Lazarus's words etched on the Statue of Liberty eloquently promise: "Give us your tired, your poor, your huddled masses yearning to breathe free." Yet as the course of the war proved, the United States slammed its doors shut to six million doomed Jews.

The sickening success of the Holocaust, though masterminded and executed by Hitler and the Nazi regime, cannot be wholly attributed to one small group's maniacal policy of racial cleansing. To Hitler's delight, the democratic, humanitarian governments contributed to the deliberate murder of two-thirds of Europe's Jews. Since the war, however, the United States has escaped condemnation for its part in a war the world has essentially viewed as a story of killer and killed. . . . Through half-hearted efforts the United States and its Allies did indeed save thousands. But other opportunities to save even more were stalled or rejected by such obstacles as ignorance, indifference, indolence, and cowardice. . . .

In August 1942, a member of the Czechoslovak State Council sent a memorandum regarding the Jews' situation to the United

States, in which he stressed the moral challenge confronting the Allies. "This war is not being waged with bombs and guns alone, nor will the nature of the coming world be determined by the outcome of battles," he wrote, urging the Allied governments not to be guilty of "grave sins of omission." Others shared his fear. Szmul Zygielbojm, a Jewish Socialist member of the Polish National Council devoted to publicizing the plight of the Jews, committed suicide in 1943, dejected over Allied indifference. Zygielbojm as well placed the responsibility for the murder of millions of Jews on "the whole of humanity." In this moral call to arms, no nation was endowed with more expectations than the United States. But of all the individuals and groups who denounced the Nazis and demanded counteraction, none were powerful enough to inspire effective retaliation. The failure of the "democratic impulse" to stir the United States to action constituted a blatant contradiction of America's altruistic image, as well as undermined the popular conception of America's beneficent role in World War II. The United States faced a clear obligation, and various groups—the press, the military, the people, the State Department, and [U.S. president Franklin] Roosevelt—all failed their responsibility to the Jews. Thus, the blood of six million Jews who perished in the most horrible, deliberate act of violence ever engineered by humankind has come to stain the hands of not only the perpetrators, but the bystanders as well.

Finding Out About Hitler's Plans

Throughout the murderous years and months of planning and executing the Final Solution [Hitler's plan to exterminate the Jews], Nazi officials worked efficiently and secretly. Few written orders or documents were ever produced regarding the Holocaust; most were issued verbally or concealed in heavily coded documents. But despite the high priority of secrecy, Nazi Germany could not long conceal a project of such a scale involving millions of Europe's inhabitants and employing so many of the Reich's resources. The average civilian easily witnessed the daily disappearance of Jews from the streets of Europe. In July 1942 alone, the Germans removed 18,000 Jews from Paris under the stated purpose of deportation to the East. That same month, the Nazis began to ship 6,000 Jews a day from the Warsaw ghetto in Poland to their death at Treblinka. Thousands were removed every day from other countries such as Belgium and Holland. As news of deportations regularly reached the Allied world, these events were common knowledge to the American and the European.

Ultimately, it was the information pushed through underground channels that culminated in the exposure of Hitler's Final Solution. This discovery drastically altered people's perceptions by replacing the suspicions of random atrocities imposed on various peoples with evidence of a systematic plan for the extermination of one people. In the summer of 1942, however, news to that effect began to emerge. In July, a document issued by the Polish government-in-exile in London reported that 700,000 Jews, mostly Poles, had been killed by the Germans since the September 1939 invasion. . . . The report entailed a "city-by-city roll call of death" in which as many as 1,000 died per day. Furthermore, Zygielbojm, whose wife and two children had perished at the hands of the Nazis, testified on the BBC that the report was true. The World Jewish Congress added that every Jew's destination was a "vast slaughterhouse" in Eastern Europe, and that since 1939, an estimated million or more Jews had been killed. These initial reports regarding the Jews' grisly fate were widely publicized.

On August 1, 1942, "history thrust a terrible burden" upon Gerhart Riegner, a member of the World Jewish Congress in Geneva, when he discovered through an informant that Hitler had ordered the deaths of all Europe's Jews. Riegner passed on the information to the State Department, which decided to suppress the report until further confirmation was obtained. In the following weeks, numerous reports substantiating the Riegner allegations materialized. . . .

Though not privy to documents crossing State Department desks, the American people were not blind to the genocide unfolding halfway around the world. The newspaper became the most prevalent medium for informing the people. David Wyman, in *The Abandonment of the Jews: America and the Holocaust, 1941–1945*, emphasized that the American press did little to publicize news of the Holocaust and stir public activism, and he blamed the press as one of the groups which failed the Jews during the war. Although coverage was sometimes scant and often relegated to inner pages, the information was still available to the American public. During the summer of 1942, newspapers acknowledged the various reports of Nazi atrocities. On June 27, for example, the *New York Times* published about two inches on page five regarding the Polish government's report, which was also broadcast on the BBC and CBS radio, of 700,000 Jews slain by the Nazis. The article quoted the statement: "To accomplish this, probably the greatest mass slaughter in history, every death-dealing method was employed—machine-gun bullets, hand grenades, gas chambers, concentration camps, whipping, torture instruments, and starvation." Three days later, a longer article under the headline "1,000,000 Jews Slain By Nazis, Report Says," appeared in the *New York Times* detailing the World Jewish Congress report.

An announcement made by Nazi Propaganda Minister Joseph Goebbels on June 12 should have sounded warning bells. In retaliation for Allied air bombings of German cities, Goebbels promised that the Nazis would execute a mass "extermination" of European Jews. He elaborated: "The Jews are playing a frivolous game and they will pay for it with the extermination of their race in all Europe and perhaps even beyond Europe." *The New York Times* carried this medium-length story on page seven. If they did not quite trust Goebbels, Americans could have listened to Hitler's speech at the Berlin Sports Palace on September 30. It was recorded on German radio and reported by American newspapers:

> In my Reichstag speech of September 1, 1939, I have spoken
> . . . that if Jewry should plot another world war in order to ex-
> terminate the Aryan peoples of Europe, it would not be the
> Aryan peoples which would be exterminated, but Jewry . . .
> At one time the Jews of Germany laughed about my prophe-
> cies. I do not know whether they are still laughing or whether
> they have already lost all desire to laugh. But right now I can
> only repeat: they will stop laughing everywhere, and I shall be
> right also in that prophecy.

After the State Department obtained confirmation of the Riegner report, Undersecretary of State Sumner Welles went to Rabbi Stephen S. Wise of the American Jewish Congress and authorized him to release the information to the press. On November 24, 1942, Rabbi Wise held a press conference in Washington and told reporters that the State Department had confirmed that two million European Jews had already fallen victim to Hitler's plan of total extermination. . . .

From that moment on, more news would point to the horrible truth of Hitler's Final Solution. November 1942 marked a turning point, as ignorance turned into awareness. Discovery should have evolved into action, but as the events of the next three years showed, it did not. . . .

President Roosevelt's Role

President Roosevelt's passivity set the tone for American wartime policy toward the Jews. "Roosevelt was not indifferent to the plight of the Jews," found [historian] Robert Dallek in his assessment of FDR, "On the contrary, Nazi crimes profoundly disturbed him, and he looked forward to the day when Nazi leaders would face the consequences of their actions. Yet at the same time, he saw no effective way to rescue great numbers of Jews from Hitler's Europe while the war continued." Roosevelt articulated what was to become the most popular excuse for avoiding moral responsibility: winning the war. American officials invoked this in two ways: one, that the Jews' situation simply did not rank high on a list of priorities cluttered by direct war aims; and two, that winning the war would best save Jews, given the difficulty of rescue and resettlement. Historians have pointed to other significant factors which helped shaped Roosevelt's policy. Foremost among these was Roosevelt's submission to public opinion; he allowed it to interfere with the welfare of helpless Jews and with the United States's obligation to attempt to save them. . . . According to historian Paul Johnson, in addition to his "purely domestic and political considerations" Roosevelt was "mildly anti-Semitic" and "ill-informed." His ignorance was reflected . . . in January 1943, when he alluded to the "understandable complaints which the Germans bore toward the Jews in Germany," citing that Jews held a disproportionate amount of professional positions.

Roosevelt's primary failure was not in purposefully preventing the rescue of Jews, but in remaining silent and failing to motivate action. Wyman concluded that Roosevelt, in failing in a sincere effort to save the Jews, committed the "worst failure" of his presidency. In the end, it was not enough; as Holocaust historian Marty Noam Penkower wrote: "The Jews could not wait for an Allied victory. Adolf Hitler would not let them wait."

On October 6, 1942, Roosevelt announced that the United States, Great Britain, the USSR, and several governments-in-exile would establish a collective War Crimes Commission to record war crimes and prepare for post-war punishment. However, the announcement was almost made without the Americans, who delayed responding to a British proposal for the Commission for two months. British Foreign Secretary Anthony Eden warned American officials that if he did not receive a response, the announcement would be made without the United States. . . . Roosevelt himself made the announcement, giving the impression to the public that the Americans secured the new commission, and not stalled its formation.

As the Nazi regime overpowers the Warsaw Ghetto uprising, SS guards round up the remaining Jews for deportation to concentration camps.

Further announcements were made throughout that winter and following spring, including a joint United Nations Declaration signed by the three major Allied governments and eight occupied countries. The essence of the declaration, issued on December 17, acknowledged Hitler's determination to "exterminate the Jewish peoples of Europe" and condemned "in the strongest possible terms this bestial policy of cold-blooded extermination." The co-operating governments indicated that post-war punishment would be forthcoming. Unlike the War Crimes Commission, this declaration dealt specifically and exclusively with the Final Solution. It was indeed a powerful statement—as powerful as a statement could be to a Jew facing death. While highly publicized announcements such as these condemning Nazi atrocities helped increase general awareness, they promised little or no immediate action and meant nothing to Jews stranded in Hitler's death trap. . . . Americans in a leadership position, such as Roosevelt . . . were able to evaluate American capabilities and objectives, and they still failed to employ as many available resources as possible to rescue Jews and other refugees, as the 1943 incident in Rumania so prominently illustrates.

The Rumanian Jews Episode and Bermuda Conference

In February 1943, the Rumanian government approached the British and Americans with an offer to move 70,000 Jews starving and dying in the Rumanian region of Transinitria to any place of refuge the Allies determined best, provided that the Allies pay shipping expenses. In this instance, the United States outright rejected an opportunity to save a number of Jews, as well as revive its already ailing reputation for humanitarianism. When [Sumner] Welles investigated the offer, he dismissed it as "without foundation." He further identified the plan as the product of the "German propaganda machine which is always ready to use the miseries of rite people of occupied Europe in order to attempt to create confusion and doubt within the United Nations." Wyman condemned Welles' cursory investigation of the report, especially for neglecting to contact directly Rumanian officials. That the plan may not have worked in the long run was irrelevant. "The crucial point is," stressed Wyman, "that against a backdrop of full knowledge of the ongoing extermination program, the American and British governments almost cursorily dismissed this first major rescue opportunity."

Fear, not hope, that authorities would release vast numbers of refugees into Allied hands steered the course of action in this incident and throughout the rest of the war years. Paul Johnson found this to be true: "The British and American governments were in theory sympathetic to the Jews, but in practice they were terrified that any aggressively pro-Jewish policy would provoke Hitler into a mass expulsion of Jews whom they would then be morally obliged to absorb." In a similar instance regarding the removal of thousands of Jews from Bulgaria, Hull approached Eden for a solution. Eden responded that if they removed the Jews from Bulgaria, "the Jews of the world will be wanting to make similar offers in Poland and Germany. Hitler might well take us up on any such offer and there simply are not enough ships and means of transportation in the world to handle them." Throughout the war, it was evident that the Allies perceived an undeniable responsibility as an unwelcomed burden. . . .

[Two months after the Rumanians' offer] delegates from the Allied governments arrived in Bermuda to discuss the refugee problem. It is the virtually unanimous assertion of Holocaust historians that the "especially criminal" Bermuda Conference of April 1943 marked the pinnacle of Allied apathy. The Bermuda Conference originated out of a British proposal to the United States asking for an informal United Nations conference to remove refugees from neutral countries, encourage those countries to accept more refugees from Nazi-occupied territory, and recommend action to the Intergovernmental Committee on Refugees [ICR]. Assistant Secretary of State Breckenridge Long, who handled all refugee questions for the State Department and wished to avoid the British overture, returned a report to the Foreign Office stating the various ways the United States "has been and is making every endeavor to relieve the oppressed and persecuted peoples." According to Long's diary, he intended for his report to show up the British on the refugee problem and make it their responsibility. . . .

Ever mindful of public opinion and more concerned about resurrecting their humanitarian image than saving Jews, American officials reopened negotiations for a two-power conference on the refugee problem. . . . Remoteness from the press and public pressure encouraged organizers to choose Bermuda as the site. . . . The delegates approached their task with reluctance and few expectations. . . .

The talks at Bermuda yielded six recommendations: 1) Hitler should not be approached for the release of potential refugees; 2) the British and Americans should acquire neutral shipping to transport refugees; 3) the British should consider allowing refugees into Cyrenaica in North Africa; 4) refugees should be removed from Spain; 5) the governments should issue a joint declaration on the repatriation of refugees; and 6) ICR should be reorganized to meet the needs of war refugees. . . .

In claiming that it thoroughly discussed the remotest possibilities, the delegation perhaps forgot the cursory attention it paid to certain avenues of rescue. During the second day of talks, the delegation immediately dismissed what it considered the "more radical proposals" submitted by Jewish organizations, including the appeal to Hitler to release Jews, the lifting of the blockade to aid persecuted people, and UN shipping for refugees. It was agreed that these subjects were both impossible and outside the scope of the Conference, stated the final report.

Bermuda was almost unilaterally denounced by contemporary critics as a "program of inaction" and a "cruel mockery." Freda Kirchwey of *The Nation* wrote that Bermuda "has brought nothing but a series of excuses for the failure of the British and American governments to do anything effective to rescue the victims of Hitler's terror who still remain alive." *The New Republic* noted that no Jewish organizations were represented at the conference, which was "purely exploratory," unable to make any decisions except to recommend action to the ICR. "Meanwhile," it read, "the hourly slaughter of Jews goes on.". . .

Losing the Moral War

Paul Johnson concluded his discussion of the Allied role in the Holocaust on "a harsh and important point." The United States did not rescue Jews because such an endeavor interfered with the war; not to help the Jews was to help defeat Hitler. Similarly, for Hitler to persist in killing the Jews, he was sacrificing thousands of his own soldiers and SS men, tons of resources, and millions of able-bodied Jews, thus contributing to an Allied victory. Hence, "the Holocaust was one of the factors which were [sic] losing Hitler the war. The British and American governments knew this," wrote Johnson. Although other factors certainly contributed to the Allied victory, such as production capabilities and superior leadership, Johnson was suggesting that the existence of a wartime mass-murder program significantly affected the outcome.

Although it is impossible to discern to what extent the multitude of variables altered the outcome of the war, most realized that for every SS man guarding prisoners in a work camp, there was one less individual to build tanks or Uboats. For every train that shipped Jews to their deaths, supplies were not reaching the front on schedule. For every bullet pumped into the body of a Jew, an American soldier could keep on fighting. By the same token, every resource that the United States withheld from the refugee effort was diverted to the war. Simple mathematics dictate that the genocide proceeding under the guise of the war secured an Allied victory, but only in the military sphere. As many articulated when they learned of the plight of the Jews, the Second World War was not to be just a military struggle. It was also a moral battle, one that both sides lost. At the crossroads of the twentieth century, the United States met the moral challenge not by wiping out the evil it confronted, but by layering its own indifference on top. The United States avoided reprobation because Hitler's unprecedented evil took center stage. But his terror does not diminish the others' sins. Americans were not cruel, or evil, or monstrous in the sense that Hitler was. They simply did not care. They abandoned their characteristic motivation, will, and creativity to respond to history's most tragic episode in the only humane manner.

Viewpoint 2

"It was Hitler who imagined the Holocaust and the Nazis who carried it out. We were not their accomplices. We destroyed them."

The United States and Its Leaders Were Not to Blame for the Holocaust

William J. vanden Heuvel

William J. vanden Heuvel, president of the Franklin and Eleanor Roosevelt Institute in Hyde Park, New York, here responds to charges by some modern critics that the United States was indifferent to the plight of European Jews during World War II. In the view of those who make these charges, President Roosevelt and other top U.S. leaders in a sense acted as accomplices to the genocide carried out by Adolf Hitler and his Nazi regime. According to vanden Heuvel, such notions are without foundation. He cites evidence to show that Roosevelt was a caring individual who sympathized with the Jews of Europe and endeavored to save as many as he could by defeating Hitler as swiftly as was humanly possible. Vanden Heuvel is especially emphatic in his attempt to refute the idea that the United States

William J. vanden Heuvel, lecture at Roosevelt University, Chicago, IL, October 17, 1996. Copyright © 1996 by William J. vanden Heuvel. Reproduced by permission.

purposely refrained from bombing the Nazi concentration camp at Auschwitz when given a chance to do so. The world would have condemned the Americans, he says, for killing the thousands of Jews then held in that camp.

For those who share Winston Churchill's judgment, and I do, that the Holocaust "is probably the greatest and most terrible crime ever committed in the whole history of the world," there can be no greater indictment than to allege complicity with that crime. There are some whose legitimate concerns over those grievous events lead them to try and make America and Americans feel guilt and responsibility for the Holocaust. They write and talk with barely a reference to the colossal military struggle known as World War II in which 67 million people were killed, where nations were decimated, where democracy's survival was in the balance. The Holocaust was part of World War II. Any discussion of the Holocaust must put events, values and attitudes in their time and place.

The scholarship that informed a documentary presented on the public broadcasting system on April 6, 1994, entitled "America and the Holocaust: Deceit and Indifference" made our country and its leaders "accomplices" to the Nazi barbarism. It is such scholarship that has caused many young American Jews to criticize and even condemn their grandparents and parents for being "passive observers" of the Nazi genocide, accepting the inference that they did not want to know what was happening to Europe's Jews, that they were so absorbed in their effort to be accepted or assimilated in American society that they chose silence rather than public outrage at the Nazi crimes, that they gave their overwhelming support to a President who was indifferent to the fate of Europe's Jews despite his knowledge of what was happening to them. Accusing the United States not only of abandoning the Jews but of complicity in the Holocaust, one eminent spokesman for this viewpoint has written: "The Nazis were the murderers but we"—and here he includes the American government, its president and its people, Christians and Jews indiscriminately—

"were the all too passive accomplices."
I am here today to offer a different point of view.

Before the Holocaust

Five weeks after Adolf Hitler became Chancellor of Germany in 1933, Franklin Roosevelt became President of the United States. Roosevelt's loathing of the whole Nazi regime was known the moment he took office. Alone among the leaders of the world, he stood in opposition to Hitler from the very beginning. . . .

[Roosevelt] never wavered in his belief that the pagan malignancy of Hitler and his followers had to be destroyed. Thomas Mann, the most famous of the non-Jewish refugees from the Nazis, met with FDR at the White House in 1935 and confided that for the first time he believed the Nazis would be beaten because in Roosevelt he had met someone who truly understood the evil of Adolf Hitler. . . .

The America which elected Franklin Delano Roosevelt its president in 1932 was a deeply troubled country. Twenty-five percent of its work force was unemployed—and this at a time when practically every member of that work force was the principal supporter of a family. The economy was paralyzed, despair hung heavy on the land. Disillusion with Europe after the sacrifices of the First World War encouraged profound isolationist sentiments. This is not the time or place to recount the accomplishments of the New Deal nor the daring, innovative leadership that brought about the peaceful social revolution that has earned the bipartisan, contemporary judgment of Roosevelt as the greatest president of this century. Let us rather discuss what was most relevant to Germany's Jews—our immigration laws and American attitudes to events in Europe.

The immigration laws of the United States had been established by legislation in 1921 and 1924 under Presidents Harding and Coolidge and by a Congress that had rejected the League of Nations and defined the new isolationism. The Congress controlled the immigration laws and carefully monitored their implementation. A formula assigned a specific quota to countries based on population origins of Americans resident in the United States in 1890. The law was aimed at eastern Europeans, particularly Russia and Poland. . . . Italians were a target and Asians were practically excluded. The total number of immigrants that could be admitted annually was set at 153,774. The two countries most benefited were Great Britain (65,721) and Germany (25,957). As the Depression took hold, President Hoover tightened regulations by mandating that no immigrant could be admitted who might become a public charge. The Depression also encouraged an unusual coalition of liberal and conservative forces, labor unions and business leaders, who opposed any enlargement of the immigration quotas, an attitude that Congress adamantly reflected. The overwhelming majority of Americans agreed with the Congress, opposing the increased admission of immigrants, insisting that refugees be included in the quotas of countries from which they were fleeing. Jewish refugees from Germany, because of the relatively large German quota, had an easier time than anti-Communist refugees from the Soviet Union. . . .

The President and Mrs. Roosevelt were leaders in the effort to help the German Jews fleeing political persecution. Mrs. Roosevelt was a founder of the International Rescue Committee in 1933 which brought intellectuals, labor leaders, and political figures fleeing Hitler to sanctuary in the United States. President Roosevelt made a public point of inviting many of them to the White House. In 1936, in response to the Nazi confiscation of personal assets as a precondition to Jewish emigration, Roosevelt greatly modified Hoover's ruling regarding financial sponsorship for refugees thereby allowing a substantially greater number of visas to be issued. As a result, the United States accepted twice as many Jewish refugees than did the rest of the world put together. . . . Roosevelt acted in the face of strong and politically damaging criticism for what was generally considered a proJewish attitude by him personally and by his Administration. . . .

On March 25, 1938, [Roosevelt] called an international conference on the refugee crisis. Austria's 185,000 Jews were now in jeopardy. The conference met in Evian, France. There was no political advantage for Roosevelt in calling for a conference "to facilitate the emigration from Germany and Austria of political refugees." No other major political leader in any country matched his concern and involvement. The Evian Conference tried to open new doors in the western hemisphere. The Dominican Republic, for example, offered sanctuary to 100,000 refugees. The Inter-Governmental Committee (IGC) was established, hopefully to pressure the Germans to allow the Jews to leave with enough resources to begin their new lives. The devastating blow at Evian was the message from the Polish and Romanian governments that they expected the same right as the Germans to expel their Jewish populations. There were less than 475,000 German and Austrian Jews at this point—a number manageable in an emigration plan that the 29 participating nations could prepare, but with the possibility of 3.5 million more from eastern Europe, the concern now was that any offer of help would only encourage authoritarian governments to brutalize any unwanted portion of their populations, expecting their criminal acts against their own citizens to force the democracies to give them haven. The German emigration problem was manageable. Forced emigration from eastern Europe was not. The Nazi genocide was in the future—and unimaginable to the Jews and probably at the time unimagined by the Nazis. National attitudes then are not very different than today's. No country allows any and every refugee to enter without limitations. . . .

By the end of 1938, Kristallnacht[1] had happened. Its impact on the Jews of Germany and Austria was overwhelming. . . .

The German Jews at last understood the barbarism of the Nazis—and that Hitler was totally in power. America's reaction to Kristallnacht was stronger than any of the democracies. Roosevelt recalled his Ambassador from Germany. For the first time since the First World War an American president had summoned home an ambassador to a major power under such circumstances. At his press conference then, Roosevelt said: "I myself can scarcely believe that such things could occur in a 20th century civilization." He extended the visitors' visas of all Germans and Austrians in the United States who felt threatened. The reaction of Americans in opinion polls showed overwhelming anger and disgust with the Nazis and sympathy for the Jews. Roosevelt remained the target of the hardcore anti-Semites in America. He welcomed them as

1. the "night of crystal," November 9, 1938, when Nazis destroyed Jews' businesses and property

enemies and in brilliant maneuvering, he isolated them from mainstream America and essentially equated their anti-Semitism with treason and the destruction of both the national interest and national defense. Recognizing the inertia, frequent hostility, and sometime anti-Semitism in the State Department, he entrusted Sumner Welles, the Undersecretary of State and a person totally sympathetic to Jewish needs, to be his instrument of action. . . .

Roosevelt from the beginning saw the larger threat of the Nazis. Hitler wanted to present Germany as the champion of a universal struggle against the Jews. Roosevelt would not let him. The President understood that he had to explain the vital interest that all Americans had in stopping Hitler in terms of their own security, at the same time protecting Jews from being isolated as the sole cause of the inevitable confrontation. He pressured the Europeans to respond to Hitler. . . .

What were Franklin Roosevelt's own attitudes toward Hitler and the Jews? Did he reflect the social anti-Semitism that was endemic in the America of that era? Contemporary Jews knew that they had never had a better friend, a more sympathetic leader in the White House. Roosevelt opened the offices of government as never before to Jews. Henry Morgenthau, Jr., Samuel Rosenman, Felix Frankfurter, Benjamin Cohen, David Niles, Anna Rosenberg, Sidney Hillman, and David Dubinsky were among his closest advisors in politics and government. Rabbi Stephen Wise, the pre-eminent spokesman for American Zionism, and his daughter Justine Polier, were personal friends of Franklin and Eleanor Roosevelt with as much access to the White House as anyone. Rabbi Wise described FDR by saying "No one was more genuinely free from religious prejudice and racial bigotry. . . ." He recalls in March, 1933 how "Roosevelt's soul rebelled at the Nazi doctrine of superior and inferior races . . ." and how in March, 1945, days before his death, Roosevelt spoke movingly of his determination to establish "a free and democratic Jewish commonwealth in Palestine."

The Holocaust: 1941–1945

The persecution of the Jews and their emigration from Germany were the prelude to the Holocaust. Nazi policy changed radically after the outbreak of war. The possibility of migration ended. Ger-

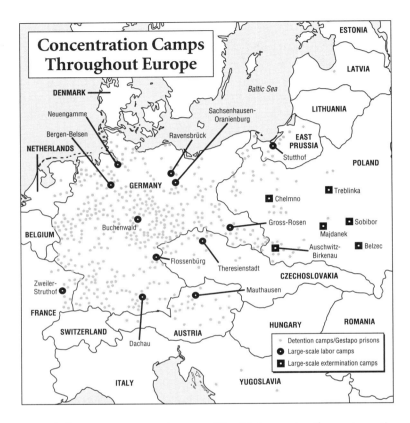

Concentration Camps Throughout Europe

many's Jews were now prisoners. The Holocaust—the systematic killing of 6 million Jews—took place between 1941–45. The likelihood is that Hitler did not expect Britain and France to go to war over Poland. . . .

As Roosevelt won an unprecedented third term as President, he—better than any American—understood what lay ahead. He had confronted the economic collapse of the United States—but recovery was slow and painful. Now he faced the political collapse of Europe, the military collapse of China—and totalitarian governments in Germany and Japan that threatened America as never before. . . . America's isolationists continued to believe that the United States was protected from harm by the two vast oceans that separated it from Hitler's Europe and Japan's militarism. President Roosevelt believed otherwise. Pearl Harbor would prove

Roosevelt's judgment correct—and give him a united country to mobilize for victory.

Hitler's conquest of the European continent let loose the full force of his psychopathic obsession about Jews. With the start of the war on September 1, 1939, emigration from Germany was prohibited. Hundreds, perhaps thousands of German Jews escaped across borders into Holland, Belgium, and Switzerland. But by June, 1940, with the fall of France, Europe became a prison for the Jews. Unoccupied France was still an escape route. Despite intense criticism from the political Left, FDR continued to maintain diplomatic relations with Vichy, France—which allowed the escape route to remain open. The International Rescue Committee—a group in which Eleanor Roosevelt remained very supportive—sent a team headed by Varian Fry which helped countless refugees—mostly Jews—find sanctuary in Spain and Portugal. But the vise was tightening. With the invasion of Russia on June 22, 1941, the lock was put on the most terrible dungeon in history. Special squads of the German SS—the Einsatzgruppen—began the slaughter of 1,500,000 Jews behind the German lines in Russia. The Wansee conference was held in the suburbs of Berlin in January, 1942. The administrative machinery was put into place for the Final Solution. . . .

The doors had been closed, not by the United States or its allies, but by Hitler. In November, 1940, the Nazi government in Poland, announcing a ban on Jewish emigration, said: "continued emigration of Jews from eastern Europe would allow a continued spiritual regeneration of world Jewry—a process urgently needed by American Jewish organizations. It is America's Jewry forcing the struggle against Germany." Similar edicts followed in all countries under Nazi control. Jews were now prisoners of a psychopath who was also the absolute dictator of Europe. On January 30, 1942, Hitler, speaking to the Reichstag, said: "This war can end in two ways—either the extermination of the Aryan peoples or the disappearance of Jewry from Europe." Since the mid-1920s, Hitler had never voluntarily spoken to a Jew. He allowed himself no contact with them. He was the most determined ideologue of racial superiority and racial conflict who ever led a country—and Germany in 1940 was the most powerful country on earth. He was more extreme than anyone around him—he was a psychopath with total power over the psychopaths who served him. . . . His central obsession, the life's mission of this deranged, monomaniacal psychopath, was to kill as many Jews as he could. Nothing diminished this mission—not the defeat of his armies, not the destruction of his country. As Germany lay in ruins, as the demented dictator prepared to end his life in his bunker in Berlin, his Nazi acolytes continued his mission above all else, diverting even urgently needed reinforcements for his retreating armies to complete the assignment of the Final Solution. . . .

Professor William Rubinstein whose book *The Myth of Rescue*, in my judgment the most important new contribution to the history of the Holocaust, states categorically that "not one plan or proposal, made anywhere in the democracies by either Jews or non-Jewish champions of the Jews after the Nazi conquest of Europe could have rescued one single Jew who perished in the Holocaust." Like all categorical statements, there are undoubtedly exceptions to what Professor Rubinstein argues but reviewing all of those proposals made between 1941–45, I believe his conclusion to be essentially correct. The prisoners of Hitler could only be saved by the total, unconditional surrender of Nazi Germany— and that was a task that required four years and the unprecedented mobilization of all of the resources, human and material, of Great Britain, the Soviet Union and the United States.

Were Rescue or Bombing Plans Feasible?

The critics of America and President Roosevelt say the news of the annihilation of Europe's Jews was deliberately kept secret so that our people would not know about it—and if Americans had been aware of the Final Solution, they would have insisted on doing more than what was done. They suggest that anti-Semitism in the State Department—or elsewhere or everywhere in our government and in our country—determined that the news of the extermination process be kept secret. That is totally untrue. President Roosevelt, Winston Churchill, General Eisenhower, General Marshall, the intelligence services of the Allied nations, every Jewish leader, the Jewish communities in America, in Britain, in Palestine, and yes, anyone who had a radio or newspaper knew that Jews in colossal numbers were being murdered. They may have received the news with disbelief. There was no precedent for it in human history. But the general information of the genocide was broadly available to anyone who would read or listen. . . . The names, locations and procedures of the death camps may not have been known—some not until the end of the war—but the fact of the genocide and the Nazi determination to carry it out were not in doubt. . . .

American Jewry was not a passive observer of these events, cowering in silence for fear of letting loose waves of anti-Semitism in America. Despite issues that bitterly divided them, primarily relating to Palestine, the Jewish community in America spoke the same words in pleading to do whatever was possible to reach out to Europe's Jews. Plan after plan was produced to rescue the Jews of Europe. Jewish leaders lobbied the Congress. Mass rallies were held across the country with overflow crowds throughout those years, praying, pleading for action to stop the genocide we now know as the Holocaust. The unremitting, remorseless massacre of the Jews—carefully concealed by top secret arrangements of the Nazi murderers—continued because no one, no nation, no alliance of nations could do anything meaningful to close down the Death Camps—except, as Roosevelt said over and over again, by winning the war and destroying the Nazis with absolute determination as soon as possible.

If Roosevelt had followed the national will, Japan would have been our military priority, but understanding the Nazi threat to civilization, he ordered Nazi Germany to be the focus of our efforts. . . . Roosevelt gave frequent audience to Jewish leaders—he sent messages to rallies of Jews across the country—he listened to every plea and proposal for rescue that came to him—but he knew that the diversion of resources from the unyielding purpose of defeating the Nazi armies might satisfy the desperate anguish felt by so many but that no one would be rescued and the rescuers in all likelihood would themselves be killed.

As Richard Lichtheim, a representative of the World Jewish Congress in Switzerland and a hero in informing the world of the genocide, said in December 1942: "You cannot divert a tiger from devouring his prey by adopting resolutions or sending cables. You have to take your gun and shoot him." Franklin Roosevelt understood that and he mobilized in America an arsenal of such strength that the world would still marvel fifty years later at how the miracle was accomplished.

The only meaningful way to save the survivors of Hitler's murder machine was to win the war as quickly as possible. . . . Consider how many more Jews would have survived had the war ended even a week or ten days earlier—and conversely, how many more would have died had the war lasted an additional week or ten days. Given the determination of the Germans to fight on to the bitter end, and knowing what Roosevelt understood then and that all of us should know now—that Hitler would never let the Jews go, that until his dying day his obsession was their destruction, that the slaughter of the Jews went on into the final moments of the Third Reich, that every day until the final surrender there were thousands of deaths by murder, starvation and disease, we should know with certainty that the number saved by winning the war as quickly as possible would be vastly greater than the total number of Jews who could be saved by any rescue efforts proposed by anyone from 1941–45.

The proposal to bomb Auschwitz has become the symbol of American indifference and complicity in the Holocaust. The War Department's rejection of this proposal on the ground that it would divert air support from the war effort was, according to David Wyman, the author of *The Abandonment of the Jews* merely an excuse. "The real reason," Professor Wyman writes, was that "to the American military, Europe's Jews represented an extraneous problem and an unwanted burden." Is there any doubt as to what George Marshall or Dwight Eisenhower would say to that indictment of America and its armed forces? For America's Jews today, I find there is nothing that disturbs them more, that causes them to question Jewish admiration of FDR more, that permits them to accept the judgment that America's passivity and anti-Semitism makes us complicitous in history's worst crime than the so-called refusal to bomb Auschwitz. Nothing is more important therefore than to review the facts.

The polemicists would have us believe that many American Jewish groups petitioned our government to bomb Auschwitz. That allegation is thoroughly wrong and discredited. . . .

Informed Jewish opinion was against the whole idea of bombing Auschwitz. The very thought of the Allied forces deliberately killing Jews—to open the gates of Auschwitz so the survivors could run where?—was abhorrent then as it is now. . . . Although only President Roosevelt or General Eisenhower could have ordered the bombing of Auschwitz, there is no record of any kind that indicates that either one was ever asked or even heard of the proposal—even though Jewish leaders of all persuasions had clear access to them both.

Every study of the military problems related to bombing Auschwitz makes one wonder what its proponents are talking about. U.S. Supreme Court Justice Powell, an ULTRA intelligence officer in World War II, when asked in 1985 about the judgment of Allied military commanders that innocent Jews should not be deliberate victims of American attacks, was incredulous that anyone would even suggest that Allied forces bomb Auschwitz. "I am perfectly confident," he responded, "that General Spaatz would have resisted any proposal that we kill the Jewish inmates in order to temporarily put Auschwitz out of operation. It is not easy to think that a rational person would have made such a recommendation.". . .

If we had bombed Auschwitz with the inevitable consequence of killing hundreds, perhaps thousands of Jewish prisoners, I have no doubt that those who defame America for inaction would denounce us today for being accomplices in the Nazi genocide. Certainly Hitler and Goebbels would have justified their madness by claiming that the Allies, by their deliberate bombing of Auschwitz, had shown their own disdain for the value of Jewish lives. . . .

The Nazis Are to Blame

The events that we are talking about—the genocide of six million Jews—was not referred to generally as "the Holocaust" until some years after the War. No one of us, including scholars and historians, can review the bestial crimes of Adolf Hitler and his Nazi thugs and all those who carried out their orders to kill innocent men, women, and children without hanging our heads in sorrow. But we must never forget that it was the Nazis who committed this most terrible crime led by a psychopath, Adolf Hitler. America—

this wonderful and generous country—was a reluctant participant in the world of the 30s. Our parents and grandparents were not fools. It was their courage and strength that made America the leader of the Free World. We should be so brave and strong—we should do so well—in our own time, with our own problems. Had Israel existed in 1939 with the military strength that it has today, the terrible story of the Holocaust might have had another outcome. Because of the Holocaust, Israel was born and America has been its unfailing supporter.

How ironic that our greatest president of this century—the man Hitler hated most, the leader constantly derided by the anti-Semites, vilified by Goebbels as a "mentally ill cripple" and as "that Jew Rosenfeld," violently attacked by the isolationist press—how ironic that he should be faulted for being indifferent to the genocide. For all of us, the shadow of doubt that enough was not done will always remain, even if there was little more that could have been done. But it is the killers who bear the responsibility for their deeds. To say that "we are all guilty" allows the truly guilty to avoid that responsibility. We must remember for all the days of our lives that it was Hitler who imagined the Holocaust and the Nazis who carried it out. We were not their accomplices. We destroyed them.

Viewpoint 3

"In a host of ways the war brought out, or underlined, the strengths of America that far outweighed its defects."

World War II Benefited America and the World

William L. O'Neill

A number of historians and other scholars argue that, although the United States made some mistakes during World War II, the nation generally fared well. In this essay, for example, Rutgers University scholar William L. O'Neill makes the case that the war effort tended to unite most Americans in a common effort and that the defeat of Nazi and Japanese totalitarianism demonstrated the strength and staying power of American democracy.

A disaster for everyone else, World War II was experienced differently by the United States. Its worse feature, the 405,000 servicemen who died of all causes, was more than offset by population growth, the total number of Americans rising from 133.4 million in 1941 to 140 million in 1945, mainly through natural increase. Sixteen babies were born for every man who died in uniform. Further, they were born into a country whose people had gained much from military spending, mean family income rising by over 25 percent in constant dollars between 1941 and 1944, a remarkable accomplishment for a nation at war.

This is not to minimize the sorrow. For those deprived of a loved one, no amount of prosperity could serve as compensation. Many individuals suffered such devastating losses, and many neighborhoods and towns as well. However, most of the boys not only returned, but were better equipped for civilian life than when they left it, tempered by war, older than their years, determined to make up lost ground. Greatly aided by the GI Bill and the surge of postwar prosperity, which they profited from, but to which they also contributed, they would go to school or get jobs, marry, and settle down. A magnificent generation in war, they would be splendid in peacetime also.

Many Wrongs Were Righted

Justice, too, would be served by the war. At the time, most Americans felt that victory had vindicated their democratic system and in many ways it had. To remain democratic, to the extent even of holding elections on schedule, while fighting a long and terrible war showed how committed Americans were to safeguarding their political rights. Moreover, American war aims were appropriate to a democracy, the nation asking for no territories, no indemnities, and, in a real sense, no revenge. America fought a generous war, and its benevolence extended afterward to rebuilding the economies of the states it had defeated as well as those of its allies. Americans could be proud of themselves, not only for winning the war but, by and large, for the way in which they won it.

America nevertheless failed to live up to its highest principles in very important ways, discriminating against refugees, Japanese-Americans, and blacks, while denying women full equality on the job and in the armed services. These faults were poorly understood at the time, and, except by the victims, too seldom censured. The experience was not wasted, even so. Blacks lost little time organizing after the war and 15 years later legalized segregation was everywhere under attack, with veterans playing a major part in its destruction. Immigration laws were revised, enabling many refugees to come here after the war ended. Ultimately even racial exclusion practices were struck down, opening the Promised Land to Hispanics and Asians on a scale undreamed of in the 1940s. Japanese-Americans had a long wait before the crime against them was acknowledged, but finally even this injustice was owned up to and restitution ordered by Congress. Women never got their due. When gender discrimination came under assault in the late 1960s it was for reasons unrelated to women's wartime contribution, which has never been sufficiently recognized.

That many wrongs were righted after the war does not excuse their commission. What it does show, however, is that American democracy was evolving. Wartime injustice was produced by the nation that was, not the nation that would be. Those Negroes and Japanese-Americans who fought for the chance to fight for their country were right, because the political system they defended with their lives was not so much an institution as a process. Jim Crow was legal in 1945, but in 20 more years it would be finished. The great thing about democracy is that it self-corrects, and in all these areas did.

Some Lessons Forgotten

Some valuable lessons were learned from the war, others quickly forgotten. The one that made the greatest impression was the danger of being unprepared and alone. When the Cold War developed, America would arm itself to the teeth and form military alliances with dozens of countries. Though moderation would have been better still, this overreaction was certainly preferable to a feeble response. The lesson of the 1930s was learned at last, even if all too well.

The mobilization muddles were not taken to heart, or even remembered for long. Everyone knows the Army was large, but few that it was not large enough, and desperately short of Wacs [women]. The manpower crisis is little remembered, the failure to enact national service not at all. The resulting lack of rotation for combat troops figures only in history books. The cost of fighting two Pacific Wars instead of having a single strategy has never been conceded. There has never been, and never will be, a movie about strategic bombing that shows it didn't work.

The structural weakness of American democracy that gave iso-lationists almost a veto over national security affairs in the pre-war era have not changed, either. This has nothing to do with civil rights and liberties, rather, it concerns the way decisions are made in a country where representatives run for office every two years, and in which the executive and legislative branches are frequently deadlocked. Public-opinion polls are more potent than ever. Congress remains reluctant to offend any interest group, or pass measures, however needed, that will cause inconvenience. The short term, even more than before, is what counts in Washington.

Bad Times vs. Good Times

One of the more striking aspects of the war was a generosity of spirit that it brought forth. Though government programs often fell short of need, volunteerism and individual effort took up much of the slack. While this side of the war is poorly documented, many remember it as a time when people helped each other out with car pools, block organizations, and simple neighborliness.

Before troops were shipped overseas, their wives often followed them from camp to camp, living in squalid conditions but sustained by each other, and sometimes by the kindness of strangers. Susan Keller, whose husband Dempsey was in Company K of the 84th Infantry Division, followed him to Louisiana, even though she had no car and an infant in arms and another on the way. The only place she could find to live was a single room with a family of five. The parents not only took Susan in but to the hospital when her second child was born, frequently looking after her children in addition to their own. Such experiences were far from rare. Americans were united in a common cause and had a sense of the country as being more than the sum of its interest groups. Whatever their faults, those Americans were, as Stephen Ambrose says, a "we" generation and knew it.

On V-J Day, Marjorie Haselton of Massachusetts wrote to her husband in China:

> You and I were brought up to think cynically of patriotism
> . . . by the bitter, realistic writers of the twenties and thirties.
> [But] this war has taught me—I love my country and I'm not

ashamed to admit it anymore. . . . I am proud of the men of my generation. Brought up like you and I in false prosperity and then degrading depression, they have overcome these handicaps. And shown the world that America has something the world can never take away from us—a determination to keep our way of life. . . . Call it Yankee ingenuity or whatever you will, it still is the one force that won the war—the thing the enemy never believed we had. That is why, tonight, I am proud to be an American and married to one of its fighting men. . . . You proved that Americans may look soft and easy going, "spoiled" by the highest standard of living in the world, yet when the hour of need came you showed them we could take it—*and* dish it out.

On the same day, Rose McClain of Washington State wrote a less militant but equally heartfelt letter to her husband in the Pacific:

Today I cried and thanked God for the end of this war and I shall continue to pray that this shall be the end of war for all time. That our children will learn kindness, patience, honesty, and the depth of love and trust we have learned from all of this, without the tragedy of war. That they shall never know hate, selfishness and death from such as this has been.

Nancy Arnot Harjan was seventeen when the war ended. She had been doing her bit, giving blood, knitting scarves and caps for the servicemen, dancing with sailors at the USO, and bringing them home for dinner. On one level she knew that most of the warriors were boys like those she dated. Yet, on another level, as she later recalled:

I saw on the news films the Parisian people, with tears streaming down their faces, welcoming our GIs. They were doing what I wanted them to do. When the Holocaust survivors came out, I felt we were liberating them. When the GIs and the Russian soldiers met, they were all knights in shining armor, saving humanity. [Laughs.] I believed in that.

The embarrassed laughter is that of the adult recalling her naive youth, yet, what she remembered thinking then was, if not the entire truth about the war, certainly true enough.

Though an exciting time for girls like Nancy, the war years were hard on women separated from the men they loved. This was true even of college students, who had fewer problems than most. Katherine McReynolds was an undergraduate at the University of Missouri who, after the war had ended and she did not have to keep up a cheerful front, wrote to her future husband overseas:

> [Our housemother] thinks we all seem so mature. Why shouldn't we? Franny's Richard and June Digby's twin brother were killed. Meyer's fiance spent six months in a German prison camp. The rest of us have been worried sick and hopelessly lonesome for years. It's a wonder we aren't old women.

There is no way to factor these elements into a comprehensive equation. How do we balance precious lives lost against those precious new lives brought into the world even as the fighting raged? The sum of human suffering, at home and on the battlefield, cannot be measured against the good times that got better and better even as the casualties rose.

The Greatest of All Tests

All one can say in the end is that the war was, and remains, well worth the effort and the heartbreak. As evidence, one has only to imagine what kind of world we would live in today if America had remained neutral. Russia might have survived in a shrunken form, and Great Britain for a time also, but the rest of Eurasia would have been enslaved by the Axis powers. The Holocaust would have gone on to its bitter end, and we can be sure that a victorious Hitler, armed soon with atomic weapons and ballistic missiles, would have caused additional havoc—dwarfing that which was actually wreaked. The most to be hoped for in that event would have been the world that George Orwell described in *1984*—at worst, no world at all.

By passing this greatest of all modern tests America also won the right to become a better nation. Though social reform was not why most servicemen took the risks they did, it would be one of the outcomes. Some reforms, like the defeat of racial segregation, would have roots in the war experience. Others would result from the democratic impulse itself that the war had been fought to preserve. In a host of ways the war brought out, or underlined, the strengths of America that far outweighed its defects. Family values were not just a political slogan but a fact of daily life. Most people married for keeps. Fathers supported their children. The war years were not an age of innocence. . . . Relations between the Allies were strained, politicians often cynical, and individual selfishness remained about the same. But, more so than now, Americans accepted responsibility for their acts and did not uphold personal gratification as the be all and end all of life. They believed in doing their duty, at home as at the front.

The most pluralistic of democracies, a Trans-National America, as the social critic Randolph Bourne had called it, this country proved that ethnic diversity enriched rather than weakened. Its fighting men met every test. Its leaders may have faltered, but did not fail. The people overcame their enemies, surmounting as well the difficulties presented by allies, a chaotic and divided government, among other faults, to gain what [Franklin] Roosevelt had promised would be "the inevitable triumph." "Sweet land of liberty," the children sang, and so it was, and so it would remain—thanks to a great generation.

Viewpoint 4

"World War II . . . has been converted over time from a complex, problematic event . . . to a simple, shining legend of the Good War."

The Benefits Brought by World War II Are Exaggerated

Michael C.C. Adams

Many people have come to think of World War II as the so-called "Good War" because it defended the world against tyranny and helped unite Americans of all walks of life in a common cause. However, some observers disagree, among them Michael C.C. Adams, a professor of history at Northern Kentucky University. In this excerpt from his book about World War II, he asserts that the Good War is largely a myth that ignores racial discrimination, battlefield atrocities, broken families, and other problems associated with the war.

All societies to some degree reinvent their pasts. This is not intended, not a pattern of deliberate lying; but too much has happened for it all to be retained in popular memory. Therefore, to make our understanding of history manageable, we try to re-

Michael C.C. Adams, *The Best War Ever: America and World War II*. Baltimore: The Johns Hopkins University Press, 1994. Copyright © 1994 by The Johns Hopkins University Press. Reproduced by permission.

trieve from the huge clutter of the past only those events that seem to be particularly useful, interesting, or exciting. Usable historical events appear to offer helpful insights into how people of the past confronted problems or situations similar to our own.

Examples of functional and engaging past happenings are dramatic disasters, such as the sinking of the Titanic, which serve as warnings, or great triumphs, such as World War II. We tend to dwell on the victories because they make us feel good about ourselves. We see them as events that showcase our national strength, collective courage, idealism, and other desirable traits.

Sometimes we conjure up the past in such a way that it appears better than it really was. We forget ugly things we did and magnify the good things. This is wishful thinking, the desire to retell our past not as it was but as we would like it to have been. If the past is remolded too drastically, it ceases to be real history. It becomes what we call myth, or folklore, instead. One task of the historian is to try to keep our knowledge of the past as complete and accurate as possible so that our popular version does not depart too far from reality. If history becomes too mythologized, it may lose its value as a tool for understanding our course as a society. Adolf Hitler presented a deeply distorted view of Germany's history and role in the twentieth century. When this was accepted by his people, they embarked on a course leading to national disaster.

The influence of historians is, however, limited. Because they must be comprehensive in their treatment of the past and cannot simply choose to highlight the exciting and dramatic, their work often strikes people as boring and tedious. It cannot compete with modern vehicles of folklore history: film and television. In addition, historians, too, are victims of the immenseness of the past: they can never read, digest, and describe all there is to know about an event or character (there are one million documents in the Lyndon Baines Johnson Library alone). They must be highly selective in what they choose to present to us, so their picture is incomplete, a distortion to some degree. And as they are creatures of their time and place, members of the society as well as professional observers of it, their retelling of history will be molded partly by the same biases and constraints that shape the popular view. Then, through repetition, people come to believe that this partial portrait is the whole landscape of history, and what is forgotten will be thought never to have existed.

An Enduring Myth

Such a process happened with World War II, which has been converted over time from a complex, problematic event, full of nuance and debatable meaning, to a simple, shining legend of the Good War. For many, including a majority of survivors from the era, the war years have become America's golden age, a peak in the life of society when everything worked out and the good guys definitely got a happy ending. It was a great war. For Americans it was the best war ever.

This was the film age, and the script could have been written in Hollywood. The original villains were the Nazis and the Fascists, many of whom obligingly dressed in black. They bullied the weak-willed democratic politicians who tried to buy them off, which gave us the word *appeasement* as a catchall term of contempt for anyone who suggests a diplomatic solution to potential international aggression. The bad guys then took the first rounds, driving opponent after opponent out of the fighting. The Americans gave material aid to their cousins, the British, who finally fought pluckily with their backs to the wall, until the United States was brought into the fighting by the treacherous Japanese, who crippled the Pacific fleet at Pearl Harbor.

For a while, it looked grim all over, but then the Allies fought back, their victories culminating in the unconditional surrender of all enemy nations, who were then made over in our image. America emerged from the war strong, united, prosperous, and the unrivaled and admired leader of the free world. . . .

The idea that World War II was the best war America had is not entirely off the mark; like any enduring myth, it rests on a solid core of credible argument. America cemented its final rise to world power with relatively light losses: about 300,000 Americans died; a further 1 million were wounded, of whom 500,000 were seriously disabled. Tragic as these figures are, they are dwarfed by those for other belligerents. The Japanese lost 2.3 million, Germany about 5.6 million, China perhaps as many as 10 million, and the Soviet Union a staggering 20 million. Put another way, the death rate in the American Civil War of 1861–65 was 182 per ten thousand population. For World War II, the proportion of Americans killed was 30 per ten thousand.

Of the major belligerents, the United States was alone in enjoying a higher standard of living as a result of the war. Following the lean Depression years, the gross national product for 1940 was $97 billion. By 1944 it had reached $190 billion. The average gross weekly wage rose from $25.20 in 1940 to $43.39 in 1945, an increase of 72 percent. The United States was unique among the principal combatants in being neither invaded nor bombed, and most people, in or out of uniform, never saw a fighting front. As a result, the war was for many a prosperous, exciting, even safe change from the "ruined and colorless landscape of the Depression," as Russell Baker, a writer who grew up in the 1930s, termed the decade. "It was," he remembered, "a season of bread lines, soup kitchens, hobo jungles, bandits riding the highways." The Depression had been a lonely time; people struggled in isolation for survival, and some committed suicide. There was, said Baker, a felt loss of love and security. World War II for a time gave Americans a sense of belonging, of community, as they were caught up in the war fever.

Most of us still agree that nazism was an evil so monstrous that the war in Europe had to be fought. "Unlike Vietnam—the war that dominated our children's lives," said 1940s veteran Roger Hilsman, "World War II was a 'good' war. Hitler was a maniacal monster, and young as we were, we saw this and understood its implications." Hilsman was correct about the need to fight. Yet he was writing with the benefit of hindsight. This is problematic, and it gives us a window through which to begin exploring what is wrong with the myth.

At the time, many Americans didn't fully understand the threat of Hitler; they wanted to beat the Japanese first because they hated them more (a 1942 poll showed 66 percent of Americans wanting the Pacific war to have priority). The Pacific campaigns were fought with a mutual ferocity that culminated in the Japanese kamikaze attacks and the Allied incendiary and atomic bombings of Japan's major cities. Many Americans of the war generation like to divorce the atom bombings from the conflict, seeing them as the curtain raiser on the nuclear age rather than the last act of our best war. But they were in fact the final destructive episode in a fight that, as historian John Ellis said, was won and lost by brute force.

The Average Amount of Selfishness

Here is the point. To make World War II into the best war ever, we must leave out the area bombings and other questionable aspects while exaggerating the good things. The war myth is distorted not so much in what it says as in what it doesn't say. Combat in World War II was rarely glamorous. It was so bad that the breakdown rate for men consistently in action for twenty-eight days ran as high as 90 percent. Soldiers of all nations performed deeds of courage, but they also shot prisoners, machine-gunned defenseless enemies in the water or in parachutes, and raped women, including their own military personnel. And they had nightmares afterward about what they had seen and done. About 25 percent of the men still in the hospital from the war are psychiatric cases.

Posttraumatic stress disorder no more originated with Vietnam than did napalm. This terrible weapon, a jellied gasoline that burns its victims, was invented by American scientists during World War II and used in all major combat zones, along with phosphorous, another flesh-searing load for bombs and shells. On all battlefronts where there were perceived ethnic differences, the war was fought without many rules. Russians and Germans butchered each other indiscriminately. The Japanese abused Allied prisoners and were in turn often seen as subhuman "gooks."

Contrary to the popular myth that dumps all negatives on Vietnam, the worst war we had, there was significant discrimination in the armed forces during World War II. Many soldiers didn't know what the war was about, and some resented their war-long terms of service, feeling they were doing everybody's fighting. The majority of returning soldiers got no parades. James Jones, a veteran, noted that wounded men repatriated to the United States were treated as though diseased, and people rushed to wash their hands after greeting them. Civilians feared that the GIs would think the country owed them a living, while veterans felt that "when you come back they treat you just like scum." Said this anonymous soldier: "If you ever get the boys all together they will probably kill all the civilians."

America's industrial output to sustain the war was prodigious. As indicators, 86,000 tanks, 296,000 planes, and 71,000 warships were produced. Many of these were of sound design and quality. Others were not. For economy and swiftness, many American aircraft carriers had unarmored flight decks, which made them vulnerable to airborne attacks. American torpedoes were of poor quality initially, until Axis designs were copied. The "mulberries," floating artificial harbors used to assist the British-American Normandy landings, functioned poorly, and the American one at Omaha Beach was wrecked by high seas. Although Joe DeChick, a local talk-show host, recently called the B-17 Flying Fortress a "lean, mean fighting machine" that "was virtually invincible," it suffered heavy losses in raids over Germany until it could be protected by new, long-range fighter planes.

After the initial post–Pearl Harbor burst of unity and willing sacrifice, Americans showed the average amount of selfishness and cupidity. Politics became politics again. The administration collected gossip about General Douglas MacArthur's sex life to use if he ran for president on the Republican ticket. And innuendos about homosexuality helped to force Sumner Welles out of the State Department when it was decided he was too pro-Soviet. Labor-management disputes continued. Merchant seamen, taking badly needed supplies to the troops on Guadalcanal, turned back when they were refused extra pay. An elderly gentleman on a bus in Viola, Kentucky, home of a munitions plant, hit a female passenger with his umbrella when she said she hoped the war wouldn't end until she had worked long enough to buy a refrigerator.

The war massively altered the face of American society. Small farmers and storeowners went under, while big businesses became great corporations. Fed by the emergency, the federal bureaucracy mushroomed from 1 million to 3.8 million. Most people paid income tax for the first time. Millions of Americans moved, usually to the cities, which experienced considerable racial tension and some violence as ethnic groups were thrown together. The stress of social change also showed up in a record number of hospital admissions for patients suffering from psychoses. Family dislocation came to be a concern: with fathers in the armed forces and mothers working, kids seemed to go wild, and people worried about juvenile delinquency. In a 1946 opinion poll, a majority of adults said adolescent behavior had degenerated during the war; only 9 percent thought it had improved. And people may now think that marriages were more sacred back then, but marital strain led to a record high 600,000 divorces in 1946.

Americans may have been better educated then, too, but a 1942 poll showed that 59 percent of them couldn't locate China, a major ally, on the map. In the same year, Philip Wylie, a disillusioned federal official, published *Generation of Vipers*, a book cataloguing America's ills. The list is startlingly modern. Young people, he said, could no longer think because education failed to challenge them—and nobody flunked. They listened to radio and watched movies instead of reading books. Teachers who were intellectually demanding got fired. Consumerism and uncritical boosterism were pervasive, making discussion of social issues like pollution, urban congestion, drug addiction, and materialism impossible. Many of Wylie's strictures were ignored at the time and have been forgotten since.

The News Manipulated

The selective process by which only positive aspects of the war received mainstream attention began during the conflict itself—one of the most censored events in modern history. Every nation rigorously edited the news. No Japanese or American newspaper, for example, carried a single report of atrocities by their own military, though there were in fact many. The beating and even killing of African-American soldiers by other U.S. service personnel also went undisclosed. Canadian correspondent Charles Lynch spoke for the whole international press corps when he said of the reporters: "We were cheerleaders." Perhaps, he thought, this was necessary for national survival in a total war. But "it wasn't good journalism. It wasn't journalism at all."

The U.S. military censored all reports from the front, and those who broke the rules were sent home. In America, the Office of Censorship vetted public and private communications, while the Office of Facts and Figures, and later the Office of War Information, published propaganda in support of the war effort. The result was a cleaned-up, cosmetically-enhanced version of reality. The war, said writer Fletcher Pratt, was reported like a polite social function. "The official censors pretty well succeeded in putting over the legend that the war was won without a single mistake by a command consisting exclusively of geniuses." When Walter Cronkite filed a report that the Eighth Air Force had blindly bombed Germany through solid cloud cover, challenging the myth that all American bombing was pinpoint accurate and hit only military targets, his copy was held up. A combat photographer who recorded the murder of SS soldiers by their American guards was told the film couldn't be screened because of technical difficulties. And when Eric Sevareid tried to broadcast descriptions of faceless, limbless boys in military hospitals, the censors told him to write about new miracle drugs and medical instruments instead.

But the news wasn't manipulated only by the censors. John Steinbeck, a tough-minded writer who exposed human misery during the Depression, admitted that as a war reporter he deliberately slanted his stories to omit anything that might shock civilians. He didn't report on the rotten conditions suffered by the infantry or on homosexual activity in the military.

Censorship in the interests of military security, even protection of civilian morale, has its purpose. But the image-making went beyond this. Generals, even whole branches of the service like the paratroops and the Marine Corps, employed platoons of public relations officers and advertising agencies to make sure they looked good. General Douglas MacArthur was a notorious publicity hound. During the first months of 1942, when the Japanese were smashing his defenses in the Philippines, he still found time to publish 140 press releases. Manufacturing an enemy body count is usually associated with Vietnam, but for one two-year period in the Pacific war, MacArthur reported 200,000 Japanese killed for 122 Allied losses. After he was driven from the Philippines, the general became famous for the line, "I shall return." But this sound bite was manufactured from his speeches by staffers. When he did return, the dramatic scenes of him wading ashore were filmed several times on different beaches to get the right effect. . . .

One of the most popular mantel ornaments of the 1940s was a set of three brass monkeys, one covering its eyes, another its ears, a third its mouth. Called See No Evil, Hear No Evil, and Speak No Evil, they represented a quite common approach to life. When the Pentagon released candid photographs of American corpses after the battle for Tarawa in the Pacific, it received piles of abusive mail demanding that such obscene disclosures be stopped. After disfigured soldiers from the plastic surgery hospital in Pasadena, California, were allowed to go downtown, the local paper got letters asking, "Why can't they be kept on their own grounds and off the streets?" An army survey of GI sexual practices overseas, including statistics on pregnancies caused, was kept secret for forty years after the war out of fear about public reaction. . . .

A Misleading Legacy

To the degree that America has simplified the complex experience of World War II, it is left with an incomplete and therefore misleading legacy. . . .

The ultimate problem of powerful myths about an idealized past is that they postulate a golden age, when things were better than they are now, a peak of efficiency from which the country has declined and which it must refoster if it is to prosper. In short, America's future lies in reclaiming its past. It is understandable that Americans should see the 1940s as this golden age. As a result of the war, America became prosperous and powerful. But no magic formula produced this scenario; it was a unique situation, produced largely by the fact that America alone of the great world powers was not a battleground. These circumstances cannot be recreated.

This is just as well, for the image of this golden age is highly selective. It leaves out the fact that America of the 1940s was wracked by change and troubled by many of the same problems that vex it now. It faced a rising divorce rate, juvenile delinquency, declining educational standards, and a loss of the traditional verities. And it did not always manage to resolve these difficulties. Americans do themselves a disservice when they assume that their predecessors did everything better than they do. Usually, those who want to return to the past are those who know too little about it. The war created problems that are even now not fully resolved, such as what to do about nuclear weapons and their threat to the future of humanity. The war highlighted racism in the culture and guaranteed that the issue of civil rights would be on the national agenda in the decades following 1945.

The past and its legacies are complex. We should consider all the ramifications of the war, not just the glorious and dramatic moments captured for us in Hollywood movies. The war was not a discrete event that ended when the last enemy surrendered unconditionally, leaving America the most powerful superpower in the world. The war was a profoundly disturbing moment in the flow of history, the after effects of which, like waves radiating out from a pebble dropped in water, continue now.

Viewpoint 5

"In retrospect, we can see clearly that World War II spawned the MICC [Military-Industrial-Congressional Complex] and that the war's long continuation as the Cold War created the conditions in which the MICC could survive and prosper."

World War II Resulted in Less Freedom in the World

Robert Higgs

Some historians and other observers feel that much of the freedom gained in the world by the defeat of Germany and Japan was canceled out by a huge rise of militarism in the United States in the form of the expanding military-industrial complex. In this article, Robert Higgs, a senior fellow in political economy at the Independent Institute, suggests that defense contractors, aided by Congress, flourished both during the war and in the postwar years to such a degree that the mutual distrusts of the Cold War (between the Soviet Union and the Western democracies) were perpetuated. In addition, Higgs maintains, much of

Robert Higgs, "World War II and the Military-Industrial-Congressional Complex," www.independent.org, May 1, 1995. Copyright © 1995 by the Independent Institute. Reproduced by permission.

the money spent by the U.S. government today on armaments remains a waste of resources and reflects a preoccupation with war rather than peace.

On January 18, 1961, just before leaving office, President Dwight D. Eisenhower gave a farewell address to the nation in which he called attention to the "conjunction of an immense military establishment and a large arms industry." He warned that "in the councils of government, we must guard against the acquisition of unwarranted influence, whether sought or unsought, by the military-industrial complex. The potential for the disastrous rise of misplaced power exists and will persist."

As Eisenhower spoke, the military-industrial complex was celebrating its twentieth birthday. The vast economic and administrative apparatus for the creation and deployment of weapons took its enduring shape during the two years preceding the Japanese attack on Pearl Harbor. It grew to gargantuan proportions during the war, then survived and flourished during the four decades of the Cold War. By the 1950s, members of Congress had insinuated themselves into positions of power in the complex, so that one is well justified in calling it the military-industrial-congressional complex (MICC) during the past 40 years.

The powerful role played by the MICC in the second half of the twentieth century testifies to a fact that has seldom been faced squarely: World War II did not end in a victory for the forces of freedom; to an equal or greater extent, the defeat of Nazi Germany and its allies represented a victory for the forces of totalitarian oppression in the Soviet Union and, later, its surrogates around the world. Hence, in 1945, we merely traded one set of aggressive enemies for another. In reality, the war did not end until the disintegration of the Soviet Union and the degeneration of its armed forces in the early 1990s. In America, the long war—from 1940 to 1990—solidified the MICC as an integral part of the political economy.

Contractors Reap Extraordinary Profits

Its antecedents hardly suggested how quickly and hugely the MICC would grow. Prewar military budgets were very small: during the fiscal years 1922–1939 they averaged just $744 million, roughly one percent of GNP. In those days, military purchases were transacted according to rigidly specified legal procedures. Normally, the military purchaser publicly advertised its demand for a definite quantity of a specific item, accepted sealed bids, and automatically awarded the contract to the lowest bidder.

Moreover, few businessmen wanted military business or any dealings with the New Deal government. When *Fortune* magazine surveyed business executives in October 1940, it found that 77 percent had reservations about doing rearmament work because of their "belief that the present administration in Washington is strongly anti-business and [their] consequent discouragement over the practicability of cooperation with this administration on rearmament."

But conditions changed dramatically between mid-1940 and late 1941. During that period, Congress appropriated $36 billion for the War Department alone—more than the army and navy combined had spent during World War I. With congressional authorization, the War and Navy departments switched from using mainly sealed-bid contracts to mainly negotiated contracts, often providing that the contractor be paid his full costs, however much they might be, plus a fixed fee. Contracts could be changed to accommodate changes in the contractor's circumstances or poor management in performing the work. In these and other ways, military contracting was rendered less risky and more rewarding. As Secretary of War Henry Stimson said at the time, "If you are going to try to go to war, or to prepare for war, in a capitalistic country, you have got to let business make money out of the process or business won't work."

Businessmen worked, to be sure, and they made money—far more than anyone had dreamed of making during the Depression. Much of the more than $300 billion the government spent for war goods and services ended up in the pockets of the contractors and their employees. According to a contemporary study, rates of return on net worth ranged from 22 percent for the largest companies to 49 percent for the smaller firms—extraordinary profits given that the contractors bore little or no risk.

Large manufacturing firms enjoyed the bulk of the business.

The top 100 prime contractors received about two-thirds of the awards by value; the top 10 got about 30 percent; the leading contractor, General Motors, accounted for nearly eight percent. The military research and development contracts with private corporations were even more concentrated. The top 68 corporations got two-thirds of the R&D awards; the top ten took in nearly two-fifths of the total.

The government itself became the dominant investor, providing more than $17 billion, or two-thirds of all investment, during the war. Besides bankrolling ammunition plants, the government built shipyards, steel and aluminum mills, chemical plants, and many other industrial facilities. Thanks to government investment and purchases, the infant aircraft industry soared to become the nation's largest, building 297,000 aircraft by the war's end. One might justifiably call this government investment "war socialism."

The "Revolving Door"

But it had a peculiarly American twist that makes "war fascism" a more accurate description. Most of the government-financed plants were operated not directly by the government but by a relatively small group of contractors. Just 26 firms enjoyed the use of half the value of all governmentally financed industrial facilities leased to private contractors as of June 30, 1944. The top 168 contractors using such plants enjoyed the use of more than 83 percent of all such facilities by value. This concentration had important implications for the character of the postwar industrial structure because the operator of a government-owned, contractor-operated facility usually held an option to buy it after the war, and many contractors did exercise their options.

The arrangements created in 1940 and refined during the next five years completely transformed the relations between the government and its military contractors. In the words of Elberton Smith, the official army historian of the mobilization, the relationship "was gradually transformed from an 'arm's length' relationship between two more or less equal parties in a business transaction into an undefined but intimate relationship." The hostility that businessmen had felt toward the government in 1940 evolved into a keen appreciation of how much a company could gain by working hand-in-glove with the military.

During the Cold War these relationships became institutional-
ized. Between 1948 and 1989, the government spent more than
$10 trillion (in dollars of today's purchasing power) for national
defense, and much of the money found its way into the bank accounts of the defense contractors, their employees, and their sup-
pliers. The procurement business remained as it had become during the war—fluid and subject to mutually beneficial adjustment.
Transactions were not so much firm deals as ongoing joint enter-
prises among colleagues and friends in which military officials and
businessmen cooperated to achieve a common goal not incom-
patible with, but rather highly facilitative of, the pursuit of their
separate interests.

Aside from the serenity that attends the spending of other
people's money, military-industrial dealings were smoothed by
the personal passages back and forth across the border between
the government and the contractors. People spoke of the "old boy
network" and the "revolving door." Upon retirement, thousands
of military officers found immediate employment with the contractors, while industry officials routinely occupied high-ranking
positions in the Pentagon bureaucracy during leaves from their
firms. It was easy to forget who worked for whom. As General
James P. Mullins, former commander of the Air Force Logistics
Command, remarked, the defense business "is not business as
usual among independent parties. This is a family affair among
terribly interdependent parties."

The families tended to do well. When Ruben Trevino and I
made a study of the profitability of defense contracting, we found
that during the period 1970–1989, the profit rates of the top 50
defense contractors substantially exceeded those of comparable
non-defense companies. This conclusion holds regardless of
whether profits are measured by the firms' accounting rate of return on investment or assets or by the stock-market payoff to
shareholders in the form of dividends and capital gains. We also
found that investing in defense contractors was not significantly
riskier than investing in comparable non-defense companies. In
short, this business has been very good to those involved in it.

Even when companies got into trouble, they could expect to be bailed out. Lockheed, Litton, General Dynamics, Chrysler, Grumman, and other leading defense contractors demonstrated that the Pentagon's propensity to protect its big prime contractors outweighed the inclination to hold them to the terms of their contracts. To subsidize the favored firms, the Department of Defense provided for subsidies to keep facilities open and to finance ongoing R&D, loans and loan guarantees, government-supplied plants and equipment, tax breaks, and strategic placement of new contracts.

The Costs to Liberty

Congress, as usual, went where the money was, Defense-related jobs served as a major determinant of congressional defense decisions for both liberals and conservatives. Members of Congress strove to steer contracts and subcontracts to favored constituents, who rewarded them in turn with lavish campaign contributions, votes, and other payoffs. Congressional micro-management of the defense program grew ever more elaborate as lawmakers grasped new opportunities to control the disposition of defense resources. Resistance to base closures, in particular, prompted the most exquisite legislative maneuvers. For more than a decade after 1977, the Pentagon found it impossible to close any large defense facility, no matter how obsolete or otherwise unwarranted. Weapons systems no longer desired by the military, such as A-7 and A-10 aircraft in the early 1980s, got extended funding, thanks to the efforts of friendly legislators.

This waste of money had many other pernicious consequences. With great corporations, powerful military authorities, and members of Congress all linked in a mutually self-serving complex, there was little incentive to end the Cold War. Not that anyone craved World War III. But wealth, position, power, and perquisites all rode on the shoulders of the MICC. The best of all worlds, then, was massive, ongoing preparation for war that would never occur. But with the nation well-prepared for war, national leaders launched more readily into military adventures like those in Korea and Vietnam, not to mention a variety of smaller projections of force abroad. Among the costs of the MICC, we might count the more than 112,000 American deaths sustained in the Cold War's hot engagements.

In retrospect, we can see clearly that World War II spawned the MICC and that the war's long continuation as the Cold War created the conditions in which the MICC could survive and prosper. America's economy sacrificed much of its potential dynamism as the massive commitment of resources to military R&D diverted them from the civilian opportunities being pursued with great success in Japan, Germany, and elsewhere. For the period 1948–1989, national defense spending consumed, on average, 7.5 percent of American GNP. The costs to liberty were also great, as national defense authorities, using the FBI, CIA, and other agencies, violated people's constitutional rights on a wide scale.

When we are tempted to look back at World War II as the "good war," we would do well to consider the full range of its consequences.

For Further Discussion

Chapter 1

1. List the main recommendations made by the 1945 Joint Congressional Committee on the Investigation of the Pearl Harbor Attack. In your view, were these recommendations sufficient to stop any future similar attacks? Why or why not?

2. Henry C. Clausen and Bruce Lee assert that serious gaffs in American intelligence were to blame for the success of the Japanese attack on Pearl Harbor. Cite three of their examples. Do you feel that Clausen and Lee have made a compelling case? Why or why not?

Chapter 2

1. Earl Warren, writing in 1942, argues that the United States cannot take the chance of trusting Japanese Americans to be loyal to the country. It is better, he says, to segregate and closely watch them. Was this a reasonable argument at the time? Why or why not?

2. Allan W. Austin argues that the American public's lack of education about Japanese American culture made Japanese Americans seem more remote from the mainstream and more likely to be distrusted. Is his argument convincing? Use examples from your own experience to support your answer.

3. In your own view, why did the U.S. government not imprison most or all Americans of German and Italian descent during World War II? Should this have happened? Why or why not?

Chapter 3

1. The editors of the Protestant journal *Christian Century* argue that the use of the atomic bomb against Japan was unnecessary. What data do they offer to support this view? Also, explain why they feel using the bomb was immoral.

2. Noted historian Samuel Eliot Morison argues that many of the Japanese militarists were reluctant to surrender even after the United States dropped atomic bombs on Hiroshima and Na-

gasaki. If the emperor had not stepped in and compelled them to accept the surrender, what, according to Morison, would have been the outcome? Cite some of the casualty figures he gives for an Allied invasion of Japan. Do you feel these figures are realistic? Why or why not?

3. What arguments does Hanson W. Baldwin give to support his view that dropping atomic bombs on Japan was unnecessary? Do you agree with him? Why or why not?

Chapter 4

1. Cite three ways, according to William L. O'Neill, in which the United States and/or the world benefited from the World War II experience.
2. Michael C.C. Adams argues that the so-called "Good War" was not as good as most people remember. Cite three reasons he gives for this assertion. Did reading his viewpoint change the way you envisioned the war? Why or why not?
3. Describe some examples of the congressional-military-industrial complex (as Robert Higgs calls it) at work today. Is this good or bad for the country? Why?

✳ Chronology

1933

Adolf Hitler becomes chancellor of Germany.

1936

July 18: The Spanish Civil War erupts. Hitler aids the Spanish fascists.

November 25: Germany and Japan become allies.

1939

March 28: The Spanish Civil War ends with a fascist victory.

August 2: Albert Einstein writes to President Roosevelt suggesting the destructive potential of atomic energy.

September 21: Germany invades Poland, initiating World War II in Europe.

September 29: The Nazis and Soviets divide up conquered Poland.

1940

May 10: The Germans invade France.

June 14: Hitler's troops march into Paris.

August 17: Hitler announces a blockade of the British Isles.

1941

June 22: Germany turns on and attacks the Soviet Union.

December 7: The Japanese attack Pearl Harbor and other locations in the Pacific and Asia, initiating the Pacific theater of World War II.

December 11: Germany declares war on the United States.

December 22: Japan invades the Philippines.

1942

April 18: James Doolittle leads a daring American bombing raid on Tokyo.

June 4: The United States defeats Japan in the strategic Battle of Midway.

1943

January 27: The first U.S. bombing raid on Germany.

May 13: German troops surrender in North Africa.

July 27–28: Allied bombers create a firestorm in Hamburg, Germany.

1944

June 6: The Allies launch the so-called D-day invasion across the English Channel and into German-occupied France.

June 19: The United States decisively defeats Japan in the battle of the Philippine Sea.

1945

February 19: U.S. Marines storm Iwo Jima, one of the island gateways to Japan.

March 9: American bombers create a firestorm that destroys most of Tokyo.

April 12: President Roosevelt dies and is succeeded by Harry S Truman.

April 30: Adolf Hitler commits suicide.

May 7: Germany surrenders unconditionally to the Allies, closing the European theater of the war.

July 16: The first atomic bomb is tested in a New Mexico desert.

August 6: The United States drops an atomic bomb on the Japanese industrial city of Hiroshima.

August 9: Another Japanese city, Nagasaki, is struck by an atomic bomb.

September 2: Japan surrenders to the Allies, closing the Pacific theater of the war.

For Further Research

Books

Mark Arnold-Forster, *The World at War*. New York: Stein and Day, 1973.

Paul R. Baker, ed., *The Atomic Bomb: The Great Decision*. New York: Holt, Rinehart, and Winston, 1968.

Winston S. Churchill, *The Gathering Storm*. Boston: Houghton Mifflin, 1948.

———, *The Second World War*. 6 vols. New York: Bantam Books, 1962.

Henry C. Clausen and Bruce Lee, *Pearl Harbor: Final Judgment*. New York: Crown, 1992.

Henry Steele Commager, *Freedom, Loyalty, Dissent*. New York: Oxford University Press, 1992.

Roger V. Daniels, *The Decision to Relocate the Japanese Americans*. Philadelphia: Lippincott, 1975.

Daniel S. Davis, *Behind the Barbed Wire: The Imprisonment of Japanese Americans During World War II*. New York: E.P. Dutton, 1982.

Herbert Feis, *The Road to Pearl Harbor*. Princeton, NJ: Princeton University Press, 1950.

Harry A. Gailey, *The War in the Pacific*. Novato, CA: Presidio, 1995.

Martin Gilbert, *The Second World War: A Complete History*. New York: Henry Holt, 1989.

Erica Harth, ed., *Last Witnesses: Reflections on the Wartime Internment of Japanese Americans*. New York: Palgrave, 2001.

194   WORLD WAR II

Fletcher Knebel and Charles W. Bailey, *No High Ground*. New York: Bantam Books, 1960.

Robert S. La Forte and Ronald E. Marcello, eds., *Remembering Pearl Harbor: Eyewitness Accounts by U.S. Military Men and Women*. Wilmington, DE: Scholarly Resources, 1991.

Walter C. Langer, ed., *Hitler Source Book* (from documents collected by the Office of Strategic Services, or OSS). National Archive, Washington, DC.

Samuel Eliot Morison, *History of United States Naval Operations in World War II*. 15 vols. Boston: Little, Brown, 1947–1962.

———, *Oxford History of the American People*. New York: Oxford University Press, 1965.

George L. Mosse, *Nazi Culture: Intellectual, Cultural, and Social Life in the Third Reich*. New York: Grosset and Dunlap, 1966.

Office of the United States Chief of Counsel for Prosecution of Axis Criminality, ed., *Nazi Conspiracy and Aggression*. 10 vols. Washington, DC: U.S. Government Printing Office, 1946.

William L. O'Neill, *Democracy at War: America's Fight at Home and Abroad in World War II*. New York: Simon and Schuster, 1993.

Gordon W. Prange, *At Dawn We Slept: The Untold Story of Pearl Harbor*. New York: McGraw-Hill, 1981.

William H. Rehnquist, *All the Laws but One: Civil Liberties in Wartime*. New York: Knopf, 1998.

Report of the Joint Committee on the Investigation of the Pearl Harbor Attack. Washington, DC: U.S. Government Printing Office, 1946.

Martin J. Sherwin, *A World Destroyed: The Atomic Bomb and the Grand Alliance*. New York: Vintage Books, 1977.

William L. Shirer, *Berlin Diary: The Journal of a Foreign Correspondent, 1934–1941*. New York: Knopf, 1941.

————, *The Rise and Fall of the Third Reich: A History of Nazi Germany*. Greenwich, CT: Fawcett, 1960.

John L. Snell, *The Outbreak of the Second World War: Design or Blunder?* Boston: D.C. Heath, 1962.

Louis L. Snyder, *The War: A Concise History, 1939–1945*. New York: J. Messner, 1960.

Ronald H. Spector, *Eagle Against the Sun: The American War with Japan*. New York: Free Press, 1985.

Jerry Stanley, *I Am an American: A True Story of Japanese Internment*. New York: Crown, 1994.

John Toland, *Infamy: Pearl Harbor and Its Aftermath*. Garden City, NY: Doubleday, 1982.

————, *The Rising Sun: The Decline and Fall of the Japanese Empire, 1936–1945*. New York: Random House, 1970.

Gerhard L. Weinberg, *Germany, Hitler, and World War II: Essays in Modern German and World History*. New York: Cambridge University Press, 1995.

Chester Wilmot, *The Struggle for Europe*. Chicago: NTC Contemporary, 1998.

Roberta Wohlstetter, *Pearl Harbor: Warning and Decision*. Stanford, CA: Stanford University Press, 1962.

Periodicals

Sarah Armstrong, "Work, Woman Power, and World War II," *Reference Services Review*, Spring 1998.

Karl T. Compton, "If the Atomic Bomb Had Not Been Used," *Atlantic Monthly*, December 1946.

Freda Kirchwey, "There Is No Alternative," *Nation*, August 3, 1940.

Tracy B. Kittredge, "United States Defense Policy and Strategy, 1941," *U.S. News & World Report*, December 3, 1954.

Louis Morton, "The Decision to Use the Atomic Bomb," *Foreign Affairs*, January 1957.

J. Saunders Redding, "A Negro Looks at This War," *American Monthly*, November 1942.

Miles Sherman, "Pearl Harbor in Retrospect," *Atlantic Monthly*, July 1948.

Norihiko Shirouzu, "Battle Scars: Decades on, a Legacy of War Still Haunts Japanese-Americans," *Wall Street Journal*, June 25, 1999.

Internet Sources

Gene Dannen, "Atomic Bomb: Decision, Documents on the Decision to Use Atomic Bombs on the Cities of Hiroshima and Nagasaki," www.dannen.com/decision.

Encyclopedia.com, "Causes and Outbreak of World War II," www.encyclopedia.com/html/section/WW2_CausesandOutbreak.asp.

Robert Higgs, Independent Institute, "World War II and the Military-Industrial-Congressional Complex," www.independent.org/tii/news/950501Higgs.html.

History Channel, "Live from Pearl Harbor," http://historychannel.com/pearlharbor/links.html.

National Archives, "The Lions' History: Researching World War II Images of African Americans," www.archives.gov/publications/prologue/summer_1997_world_war_two_images.html.

PBS, "Children of the [Japanese American Internment] Camps," www.pbs.org/childofcamp/history.

Ashley Smith, "World War II: The Good War?" www.isreview.org/issues/10/good_war.shtml.

University of Arizona, "Rosie the Riveter and Other Women World War II Heroes," www.u.arizona.edu/~kari/rosie.htm.

✵ Index

✳ About the Editor

Historian and award-winning author Don Nardo has written or edited many books for young people about American history, including *The Bill of Rights, The War of 1812, The Mexican-American War, The Great Depression, Pearl Harbor*, and biographies of Thomas Jefferson, Andrew Johnson, and Franklin D. Roosevelt. Mr. Nardo lives with his wife, Christine, in Massachusetts.